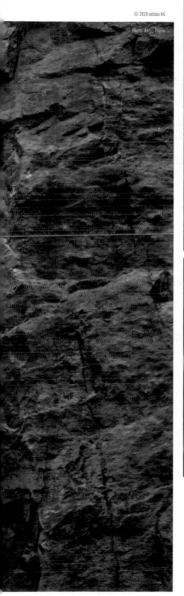

Photo: Angie Payne

Photo: Keith Ladzinski

Photo: Angie Payne

CONTENTS

Front Cover: A very near miss on Polar Circus in Alberta, Canada. Photo by Alex Ratson.
Back Cover: Rescue below Hallett Peak, Rocky Mountain National Park, CO. NPS Photo.

© 2020 The American Alpine Club

ISBN: 978-1-7356956-0-0; (e-book) 978-1-7356956-1-7. Manufactured in the United States. Published by the American Alpine Club, 710 Tenth Street, Suite 100, Golden, CO, 80401.

WARNING!
The activities described within Accidents in North American Climbing (ANAC)—including but not limited to: rock climbing, ice climbing, mountaineering, backcountry skiing, or any other outdoor activity—carry a significant risk of personal injury or death. The owners, staff, contributors, and volunteers that create this publication recommend that you DO NOT participate in these activities unless you are an expert, have sought or obtained qualified professional instruction or guidance, are knowledgeable about the risks involved, and are willing to assume personal responsibility for all the risks associated with these activities. ANAC and its publisher, the American Alpine Club, MAKE NO WARRANTIES, EXPRESSED OR IMPLIED, OF ANY KIND REGARDING THE CONTENTS OF THIS PUBLICATION, AND EXPRESSLY DISCLAIM ANY WARRANTY REGARDING THE ACCURACY OR RELIABILITY OF INFORMATION CONTAINED HEREIN. The American Alpine Club further disclaims any responsibility for injuries or death incurred by any person engaging in these activities. Use the information contained in this publication at your own risk, and do not depend on the information contained herein for personal safety or for determining whether to attempt any climb, route, or activity described herein. The examples/stories contained herein are anecdotal and/or informational only and are not intended to represent advice, recommendations, or commentary on appropriate conduct, standards or choices that you, the reader, may make regarding your own activities.

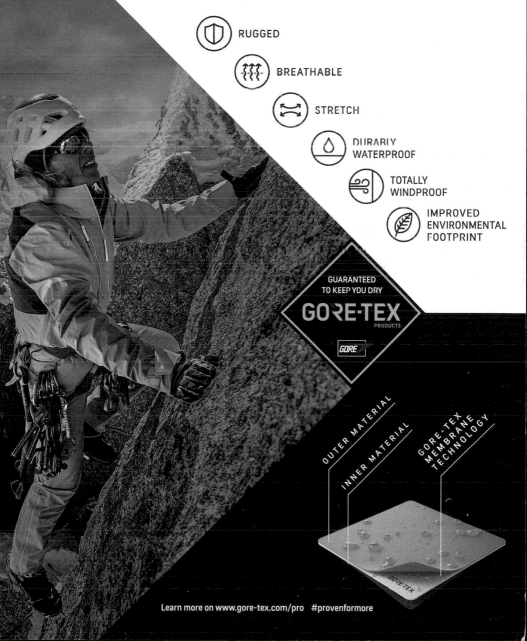

THE NEXT LEVEL OF
GORE-TEX PRO
GARMENTS

When you're battling icy conditions during a multi-day, multi-pitch climb, or caught in a torrential rainstorm two days out from basecamp, you need gear you can rely on. GORE-TEX Pro garments are built to be rugged, meaning you can rely on your gear to last from one adventure, and season, to the next – designed with an improved environmental footprint and tested to master the most extreme elements.

RUGGED

BREATHABLE

STRETCH

DURABLY WATERPROOF

TOTALLY WINDPROOF

IMPROVED ENVIRONMENTAL FOOTPRINT

GUARANTEED TO KEEP YOU DRY

GORE-TEX PRODUCTS

GORE

OUTER MATERIAL

INNER MATERIAL

GORE-TEX MEMBRANE TECHNOLOGY

GORE-TEX

Learn more on www.gore-tex.com/pro #provenformore

FIVE TEN
HIANGLE

Molly Mitchell at Cascade Canyon, Durango, CO
adidas.com/fiveten

Hypoxia is one of many dangers on the way to the summit.

Let COROS VERTIX monitor your oxygen saturation even while you sleep.

ACCIDENTS IN NORTH AMERICAN CLIMBING

Volume 12 | Number 1 | Issue 73

American Alpine Club

EDITOR EMERITUS
John E. (Jed) Williamson

EDITOR
Dougald MacDonald

MANAGING EDITOR
R. Bryan Simon

CONTRIBUTING EDITORS
Aram Attarian (Southeast), Dave Weber (Alaska)

REGIONAL EDITORS
Daniel Apodaca (Southwest); Lindsay Auble (KY &
TN); Mark Berenblum (Upstate NY); Dan Cousins
(New England); Ashton Johnston and Bill Kinter
(CO); Lauren DeLaunay, Michael Habicht, and
Christy Mohler (CA); Stacia Glenn (WA); Molly
Herber and Bret Rhinesmith (WY); Gary O'Brien
(ID); Eric Ratkowski (Shawangunks, NY); Michael
Wejchert (NH); Sarah Wolfe (UT)

DESIGN
David Boersma – Mojave Creative Lab

ADDITIONAL THANKS
Christine Blackmon, Holly Chen, Will Gadd,
Leo Paik, Jim Pasterczyk, Matt Schonwald, Deb
Simon, Grant Statham

Alpine Club of Canada

CANADA EDITOR
Robert Chisnall
anam@alpineclubofcanada.ca

PREFACE

By Dougald MacDonald

The year 2020 has been wild and unpredictable, and this publication and its parent, the American Alpine Club (AAC), have not escaped the turmoil affecting many organizations. For a long time, it seemed the financial impacts of COVID-19 would force us to skip a year in our 73-year tradition of printing this book. However, with the generous assistance of Adidas Outdoor, we have been able to print and mail the book as usual. And thank goodness, because the lessons within these pages are more needed than ever, as climbing continues to grow and more newcomers head to the hills without traditional mentorship.

The number of accidents we record has grown over the last couple of years, topping 200 in the U.S. for only the second time in our publishing history (though, on average, fatalities have remained steady). I caution readers to avoid leaping to conclusions about these numbers. For one thing, we have significantly expanded our corps of volunteer regional editors (now totaling 19 people), and their diligence and local reporting have helped us document many accidents that might have been missed in years past. Nonetheless, the accident rate does appear to be on the increase.

One disturbing trend in this year's book is a surge of anchor failures, attributed to mistakes by inexperienced and veteran climbers alike. All of these incidents resulted from unchor pieces (cams and nuts) pulling out of rock or anchor slings failing or coming untied. The key takeaway is that the strength of an anchor's components is more important than the precise (and much-debated) details of an anchor's configuration. Bomber pieces equal a bomber anchor.

In order to share more accident lessons and trends than we can with this annual publication, we have launched the monthly *Accidents Bulletin*, sent for free to all AAC members (and also supported by Adidas Outdoor). If you're not seeing the *Bulletin*, please update your email preferences at the AAC website. If you have ideas for topics you'd like us to address, email us at *accidents@americanalpineclub.org*.

Meanwhile, we're looking forward to a calmer and safer year ahead.

Submissions

Share your story and help fellow climbers! Visit *publications.americanalpineclub.org* to file an accident report online. Or email us at *accidents@americanalpineclub.org*.

Rescue Benefits

The AAC is continuously working to improve members' rescue benefits. See the latest developments at *americanalpineclub.org/rescue*.

Friends of Accidents in North American Climbing

The following people donated $200 or more in 2019 specifically to support *Accidents in North American Climbing*. Thank you! Make your own contribution at *americanalpineclub.org/donate*.

Anonymous
Stuart & Marcella Bernstein
Charles Eiriksson Jr.
Eric Frisch

Eric Green
Yannick Gingras
Richard E. Hoffman M.D.
Kurt Lustgarten

Mike McWherter
John & Rebecca Soebbing

Left to right: Wet snow avalanche on the Breithorn, Switzerland. *Matt Schonwald* Serac fall on La Meije, France. *Ian Poll* Debris below Mt. Shuksan, North Cascades, Washington. *Matt Schonwald*

Know the Ropes

AVALANCHES AND CLIMBING

Spring and summer hazards for mountaineers

BY MATT SCHONWALD

Last June I was guiding three people for a ski descent of the Coleman-Deming Route on Mt. Baker. Wind the previous day had exceeded 20 mph, loading fresh snow onto the Roman Wall, the 40° headwall before the summit plateau. I first guided this route in 1999 and knew this slope had seen multiple avalanche accidents, including the first recreational avalanche fatalities in Washington, when five people died in July 1939, entombed in the crevasses below the wall.

We skinned up from our 6,000-foot camp, with an icy wind blowing down from the summit. The new snow was soft and ankle deep, but the wind concerned us—would we have a serious avalanche issue with just eight inches of fresh in June? There was ample precedent: All of Mt. Baker's climbing avalanche victims have been killed in May, June, or July. Three hours passed and we arrived at the Coleman-Deming Saddle, just above 9,000 feet. I could see several parties descending from the Roman Wall.

I approached a guide I knew to ask why they were heading down. "A party of three took a 300-foot ride," he said. "They triggered a slab just below the top of the wall. Luckily, no injuries." Clouds swirled around the wall and no one could see the full extent of the crown. As we turned to descend, someone asked if we could still go up, since the headwall already had slid, and I took a second to respond. Did they not see the snow was unstable? That the climbers who were caught were lucky they had walked away with their lives and no injuries? I realized there was a real lack of understanding among some mountaineers that summer storms can deposit new snow deep enough to avalanche—and that even a small slide can be deadly.

A SERIOUS THREAT

Although a large majority of avalanche fatalities occur in the winter months, avalanches are not uncommon in the long days of late spring and early summer. According to a national database compiled by the Colorado Avalanche Information Center (CAIC), since 1951 in the United States, 39 out of 44 avalanche fatalities in June and 31 out of 43 in May have involved climbers.

Most backcountry skiers and winter mountaineers in avalanche-prone areas have some knowledge of the hazards and carry basic avalanche safety equipment, such as transceivers, probes, and shovels. Many seek formal training in avalanche avoidance and rescue. But preparation for avalanche hazards in the spring and summer mountaineering season is not as widespread or systematic. Most avalanche training is skewed toward winter travelers, and many avalanches that affect mountaineers occur in terrain not covered by avalanche forecasts or after avalanche centers have shut down for the season.

At the same time, the consequences of an avalanche are at least as great for mountaineers in spring and summer as they are during the winter months. As the winter snowpack melts back, additional hazards are exposed. Cliffs, narrow couloirs, exposed crevasses or boulder fields, and other terrain traps make an encounter with even a small avalanche potentially fatal.

Mountains big and small possess the potential to bury or injure you with the right combination of unstable snow, terrain, and a trigger—often someone in your party. It's not only important to recognize these hazards but also to have the discipline to respect the problem and choose another route or wait till the risk decreases. In preparing to enter avalanche terrain, the mountaineer must be focused more on avoiding avalanches than on surviving one, and that is the focus of this article.

TRAINING AND EQUIPMENT

In North America, the sequence of avalanche education for recreationalists consists of a one-hour awareness class, a three-day Level 1 course for beginners, a one-day rescue course to improve the skills learned in Level 1, and a three-day Level 2 program for amateur trip leaders, such as those leading groups of friends on a hut trip or overnight climbs. Basic avalanche training helps develop understanding of the risks a particular route might present. A Level 2 course teaches trip planners to assess problems in unfamiliar mountains and in the absence of regular avalanche forecasts.

An avalanche rescue course teaches you how to locate and rescue climbers buried in a slide. Mountaineers must be prepared for the possibility of multiple burials, since avalanches in glaciated terrain and on popular routes have a high probability of catching more than one climber. You can find courses through *avalanche.org* in the United States and *avalanche.ca* in Canada.

Some mountaineers leave behind their avalanche safety equipment during the spring and summer season, assuming the relatively stable snowpack decreases avalanche hazard. But, as we will see, there are many reasons avalanches may occur during prime mountaineering season, and safety gear—shovel, probe, and avalanche transceiver—should be used if there is any risk of being caught and buried. (A shovel and probe have multiple other uses, including leveling tent platforms and probing for crevasses.) These should be individual gear items—sharing any of this equipment reduces your ability to be located quickly or to dig out your friend.

Again, given the dangers that even very small avalanches present to climbers, recognizing the hazards and planning to avoid them is the number one survival strategy.

AVALANCHE TYPES

Mountaineering avalanches typically happen in terrain steeper than 30°, above treeline (often on glaciers), and in areas subject to winter-like storms. In other words: the terrain that climbers love. In the spring and summer seasons, when mountaineering activity peaks, climbers may face exposure to:

- **Significant storms** leaving more than a foot of new snow on your route
- **Strong winds** (>15 mph), transporting snow and building slabs on leeward slopes
- **Strong UV (solar) radiation**, increasing the risk of triggering wet loose and slab avalanches

Understanding the basic mountaineering avalanche types helps us recognize the hazards we face and our potential solutions to mitigate or avoid the problems.

Loose Snow Avalanches These slides, also known as sluffs, frequently occur as point releases (describing how they start from a singular point and then fan out and entrain surface snow, gaining mass and speed as they accelerate downhill). They can be dry or wet. "Dry Loose Avalanches" occur during or after cold winter storms with periods of rapid snowfall (greater than one inch an hour). "Wet Loose Avalanches" result from warming of the snow surface above freezing, loosening the bonds of the snow grains and creating instability; these may be triggered by falling rock or ice. Even tiny loose snow avalanches are dangerous to climbers—more so than skiers—because they can knock us off balance in very unforgiving terrain. Any avalanche is a serious threat.

During the spring and summer, the intense UV radiation from the sun makes wet loose avalanches fairly predictable, as the slopes that heat first will be southeast-facing and the hazard then moves around the mountain like a sundial. Avoiding these slides requires planning your outing so you're not on a snow slope that you need to travel up or down, under, or across when the sun hits, whether during the climb or the descent. Watch out for soft surface snow that moves easily, and try to cross slopes near or at the top to avoid being swept by heavy, wet debris.

Slab Avalanches occur when cohesive snow rests on a weak layer. If that weak layer fails, the cohesive snow fractures and cracks propagate outward, forming distinct areas that may slide. Slabs are formed from storm snow, which can happen any time of year in high alpine terrain. Wind may build deep slabs on leeward slopes, and warm spring and summer weather can add water to them, making them denser and harder to trigger yet more dangerous when they fail. Spring or summer storms that drop more than one foot of snow, followed by a clear, sunny day, are particularly hazardous. The denser snow near the surface destabilizes the slab and makes it prone to triggering, naturally or artificially.

Wind slabs will form when strong (15+ mph) winds move loose snow into dense layers. Strong winds during storms can turn six to eight inches of new snow into one- to two-foot slabs on leeward slopes such as the Roman Wall on Mt. Baker in the Cascades or Tuckerman and Huntington ravines in New Hampshire, to name a few.

For avoiding slab avalanches, it's critical to recognize red flags in the recent weather history and forecasts, as is placing camps in appropriate areas before or during storms. Climbers should wait 24 to 48 hours before attempting a route that has had more than a foot of new snow, on a leeward aspect, and/or with exposure to terrain traps.

Late spring slab avalanche in Rocky Mountain National Park. The boot track on the left was made one hour earlier. *Dougald MacDonald*

Cornice Falls create risks for climbers moving along snow ridges or failing to notice a cornice when they arrive on a snowy summit. A cornice collapse also can trigger a slab avalanche on the slopes below. The only solution is to avoid climbing under them or approaching too close, especially during the heat of the day when temperatures are near freezing.

Icefall Avalanches result from a portion of a serac or ice cliff failing in a steep, unstable glacier (think: Khumbu Icefall), creating falling ice hazard. As with cornices, falling ice presents the threat of triggering deep slab avalanches that can run far down a mountainside, threatening camps placed too close to large faces. The random nature of icefalls makes predicting these events very difficult, so the only prevention is to minimize travel time through or under icefalls, especially during the daytime, and to avoid placing camps with exposure to collapsing ice. Learn to measure the "alpha angle" below a peak or face to estimate how far debris from a large avalanche may flow (a good resource is *wildsnow.com/10011/alpha-angle-avalanche-safety*).

Glide Avalanches occur after a long period of warming, when running water has lubricated the slope underneath the seasonal snowpack, causing it to move downhill. This movement creates glide cracks, which run through the snowpack from the surface to the ground. Large and destructive glide avalanches may be the result. Glacier-polished slabs in the alpine are particularly susceptible to this problem, requiring route selection and trip planning to limit your exposure.

RECOGNIZING TERRAIN HAZARDS

Most of the "50 Classic Climbs" that are not rock climbs—along with countless other North American mountain routes—offer some seasonal avalanche hazard. In addition, the sheer vertical relief of many alpine objectives makes the possibility of a small avalanche a significant hazard. Many routes cross hanging snowfields with exposed or feature-ridden runouts. Very small loose wet avalanches can travel great distances, entraining loose snow and growing dramatically. You can travel on a valley glacier and still risk burial by these events, because faces over 3,000 feet can turn a small sluff into more than 10 feet of debris.

As you plan a climb or move up a route, look for route features that either make avalanches more likely or increase the hazard of a slide. These include:

- **Convexity:** Areas where the slope angle increases suddenly—these are places where the tension in the slope will be at its highest, making an avalanche more likely to be triggered
- **Concavity:** Areas where the slope angle decreases suddenly are also a zone of stress, due to an entire slope held up at this rapid transition from steep to flat
- **Slopes with rock features** poking through the surface, which can make triggering a storm slab more likely
- **Seracs** or **cornices** above a slope—these large, unstable features can injure you or trigger large avalanches
- **Cliffs** below steep (greater than 30°) slopes, creating exposure to small avalanches pushing climbers over the edge
- **Crevasses** below a slope, increasing the chance of a deep burial and fatal outcome

Canada has developed a system to rate terrain based on the exposure to avalanches a party will experience while moving through an area. The Avalanche Terrain Exposure Scale (ATES) is used by Parks Canada, Avalanche Canada, the New Zealand national parks, the Pyrenees in Spain, and in guidebooks and maps published by Beacon Books in the United States.

THE AVALANCHE TERRAIN EXPOSURE SCALE (ATES)		
Description	**Class**	**Terrain Criteria**
Simple	1	Exposure to low-angle or primarily forested terrain. Some forest openings may involve the run-out zones of infrequent avalanches. Many options to reduce or eliminate exposure. No glacier travel.
Challenging	2	Exposure to well-defined avalanche paths, starting zones, or terrain traps; options exist to reduce or eliminate exposure with careful route-finding. Glacier travel is straightforward, but crevasse hazards may exist.
Complex	3	Exposure to multiple overlapping avalanche paths or large expanses of steep, open terrain; multiple avalanche starting zones and terrain traps below; minimal options to reduce exposure. Complicated glacier travel with extensive crevasse bands or icefalls.

On popular mountaineering routes across North America, from Mt. Hood to Mt. Washington, and from spring routes in Colorado and the Tetons to the classics of the Canadian Rockies, steepness, exposure to multiple avalanche paths, and sometimes glaciation put most routes in the "complex" ATES rating. Such routes generally share three characteristics making avalanche accidents more common:

- Ascents in features such as gullies, couloirs, or large faces where there is no safe way to avoid exposure to avalanches
- Approaches through terrain traps with unavoidable exposure to overhead avalanche terrain, such as creeks, cliffs, moraines, moats, and crevasses
- Descents via a different route where conditions are substantially different

Recognizing and acknowledging that your route travels in "complex" terrain should prompt you to focus on identifying the areas of greatest exposure, as well as decision-making points along the route, where you can stop and evaluate the likelihood of avalanche activity.

PLANNING THE CLIMB

Planning a safe climb requires identifying areas of exposure on your chosen route and linking the prevailing conditions and forecast to an increase or decrease in the avalanche possibilities.

I use a process that starts with a weather and avalanche forecast (if available). I look at wind, precipitation, and freezing levels, as well as the recent past events from local weather stations. Then I evaluate which terrain is likely too exposed, given the current conditions, and look for routes or peaks where I can avoid unnecessary exposure. With this information, I draw up time plans for various options to get out and climb safely. Let's go into some detail on these tools, and then I'll give an example of the planning process below.

Avalanche Forecasts An avalanche forecast or bulletin gives you information regarding the avalanche hazard rating, avalanche problems, recent events such as observed avalanches on a specific slope, snowpack synopsis, and weather affecting the possibility of triggering an avalanche. The main difference between a forecast and a bulletin is the frequency they are issued—forecasts are daily, and bulletins are issued several times a week (at most). The forecast/bulletin will discuss the avalanche problems and show where they are located (distribution), size (how destructive), and likelihood of triggering (are you feeling lucky, punk?)

Most avalanche forecasts are issued from Thanksgiving through April, but most mountaineering avalanche accidents occur outside this period. The local avalanche center also may issue bulletins or seasonal recommendations giving general advice for the mountaineering season. More recent updates can be obtained from rangers, climbing guides, and the general climbing community in the area. Before a trip, visit local blogs (such as the Denali or Rainier rangers' blogs), guides' reports (such as the ACMG guides website *mountainconditions.com*), or community outlets such as regional forums and Facebook groups to get a general sense of conditions and perhaps even specific reports from your planned objective.

Weather Conditions When seasonal avalanche centers aren't issuing forecasts, it's up to climbers to use the nearest mountain weather forecast to help predict avalanche problems. Forecast sites I use include Noaa.gov, Windy.com, Mountain-Forecast.com, Meteoblue.com, and Spotwx.com; it's worth learning to use several forecasting sites. The accuracy of mountain forecasts drops off dramatically after 24 to 48 hours, so it is a good idea to check the forecast daily at least a week before your trip to see the overall trend: stormy, warm, etc. Key data to look for when checking the forecast includes:

- **Freezing Level** This tells you where snow will start to accumulate and where avalanche problems will develop.
- **Precipitation Totals** This often will come in inches of water (or millimeters outside

the U.S.) for a 6-, 12- or 24-hour period. (A rule of thumb is that one inch of water equals one foot of snow in temperatures near or below freezing.) Precipitation intensity tells you how fast slopes will get loaded; a rate of one inch or 2.5 cm (25 mm) of snow per hour is considered high intensity.

- **Wind** The predominant wind direction tells you which slopes will get loaded—e.g., southwest winds will load northeast (leeward) slopes. Pay attention to sustained wind speeds over 15 mph and duration over two hours, which may enhance the formation of wind slabs.

Remote Weather Station Telemetry You can access online data about the snowpack and recent snowfall from remote SNOTEL sites across North America. (Find links to SNOTEL locations at *wcc.nrcs.usda.gov/snow/* or on local avalanche center websites.) You can look at a full season or just a few weeks of weather history.

In the spring and summer, the snowpack typically goes through multiple melt/freeze cycles, potentially leading to avalanche problems. Early spring (March to mid-April in North America), when the snowpack is just beginning to warm up, is a very dangerous period, as old weak layers can be reactivated, leading to large, destructive avalanche cycles in alpine zones. Key red flags to research and observe include:

- **Persistent weak layers**, such as melt/freeze crusts, within the top three feet of the snowpack
- **Early warm-ups** when the winter snowpack has not adjusted to the extra heat input from longer days
- **Temperatures above freezing** for 24 hours in starting zones. If slopes don't freeze, the chances of wet avalanches go up dramatically.
- **Large rainstorms** (greater than one inch of water in 24 hours)

Time plans help you figure out what time you need to leave camp in order to safely travel up and down your route and to avoid hazards that increase in likelihood as the day warms. Web-based planning tools such as Caltopo and Hillmap offer the ability to measure distance and vertical gain on your planned route. With this information, you can estimate how much time it will take to go up and back.

I use a method I learned from the NOLS *Wilderness Guide*, in which you plan an hour for every 1,000 feet of climbing, plus rest breaks. Other systems include the Naismith Rule and the Munter Formula, which takes into account terrain and travel method. The Guide Pace app will do the calculations for you. Whichever technique you learn, a time estimate will help you determine when to start the day, especially when there are definitive spots on the route you must reach by certain times.

PUTTING IT ALL TOGETHER

A good route to examine is the Disappointment Cleaver on Mt. Rainier, as it possesses an enormous volume of objective hazards as well as a history of avalanche accidents, including the deadliest climbing avalanche in Washington history, when 11 were swept away and killed in June 1981.

Before a planned climb in the third week of June, I watched weather forecasts and noticed that temperatures had been cooler than normal and it had rained in Seattle the first two weeks of the month. Low temps and rain at sea level would mean snow up high. I checked the weather stations and saw that several feet of new snow fell between June 8 and 12, with strong winds at Paradise (5,400 feet) and Camp Muir (10,000 feet). Along with the regular climbing challenges, I added wind slabs and loose wet avalanches to my risk assessment and planned to make snowpack observations a part of my travel plan.

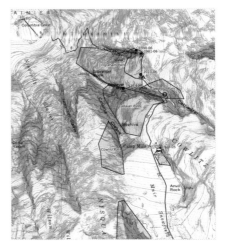

The first day on the Disappointment Cleaver route, from the Paradise parking lot to Camp Muir, gains 4,600 feet over 4.5 miles. I estimated our travel time at 5 hours 15 minutes (4.5 hours of movement plus three 15-minute breaks). Our first break will be below Panorama Point, giving us a chance to evaluate slopes that frequently are loaded after new snowfall and wind.

Planning map created on CalTopo for the Disappointment Cleaver on Rainier, showing hazard zones and rest stops. *Mall Schonwald*

Day two on the DC route gains 4,400 feet and another four miles or so to the summit. The time plan might seem like it should be close to day one's plan, but roped glacier travel, crevasse hazards, and the higher altitude will slow us down, so our travel time might be closer to six to seven hours to the summit, then three to four hours back. Timing matters, because right out of camp we will travel under the upper headwall of the Cowlitz Glacier. The aspect is southeast, requiring us to consider our return time if there is enough fresh or soft snow to entrain large debris with wet loose activity. There are three more avalanche paths to cross along the route, exposing us six more times to slides (going up and down). We'll try to reach the summit by 7 or 8 a.m., so we can be back down by 10:30 or 11 a.m., greatly reducing our chance of being under sun-baked slopes.

My map is marked with the route and rest points, along with known avalanche terrain, so I can plan where to stop and make snowpack and terrain observations. A crucial decision point is Ingraham Flats, where I can assess the Ingraham Glacier and Disappointment Cleaver before entering the last big avalanche exposure and the one with the most history. Many ghosts remain in the crevasses here.

ALTERNATIVE PLANS

An essential step in the planning process is considering alternatives. Make a list of possibilities on the same peak or in the same area to maximize your options as conditions come into focus in the last 24 to 72 hours before your climb. If the conditions don't look good, it's time to choose an alternative.

What often causes problems at this point is that big climbs are planned days, weeks, or even months in advance. Climbers may travel thousands of miles to climb a specific peak or route, only to find that conditions aren't right, despite it being the traditional "ideal" climbing season. A warm winter followed by a cold wet spring can lead to lingering avalanche problems well into June and July. Large summer storms can drop several feet of snow in the high alpine. The mountain weather does not know how much preparation and sacrifice you have put into this trip—being humble means seeing the conditions for what they are and not what you wish them to be.

RED FLAGS ALONG THE ROUTE
Sometimes, even when the forecast and conditions reports are positive, red flags may appear immediately before a climb, during the approach, or at camp the night before:

- **Recent avalanche activity** is Mother Nature's number one sign of instability. Observe the aspect and elevation of slides (similar to your route?) and other characteristics (how big? what layer slid? what type of avalanche? human or natural trigger?).
- **Lack of overnight freeze** to stabilize the snow
- **Rapid warming** (temperatures fast approaching freezing); watch for roller balls
- **Heavy rain** on steep (>30°) slopes
- **Isothermal snow**, i.e. crotch-deep wet snow, with no cohesion
- **Storm snow** greater than 12 inches (30 cm) in 24 hours and/or precipitation intensity of greater than one inch per hour. Shooting cracks or whumpfing (rapid collapse of the snow under foot) are signs of unstable storm snow.
- **Wind speed over 15 mph** during a snowstorm, creating wind slabs. These will feel denser than the surrounding snow in the lee of large boulders or cliffs.

RESPECT THE PROCESS
If red flags are observed or develop while you're on a climb, it's time to consider an alternative route or a nearby peak with less avalanche exposure. Perhaps your schedule allows time to move to a drier part of the range. On expeditions, red flags may mean waiting or even abandoning your climb while other teams go up. Trusting the process requires not believing that other groups know something you don't; many times these other parties are driven by various human factors often found in accidents.

Human factors that contribute to poor decision-making include the Dunning-Kruger Effect, in which people overestimate their knowledge and ability in the face of complex problems. We're also prone to attributing "expert" status on people moving through an area we're not sure about, in order to avoid the doubts we may feel. We may feel time pressure leading to overconfidence ("we're here, so let's just do it").

Such cognitive biases impact your ability to identify risk and consequences. It's the reason you may continue up a climb despite staring at multiple red flags. My personal trick to keep bias in check is to treat all climbs as predators that are hunting me. If I can't be confident that I will avoid becoming their meal, I back away.

The most important avalanche safety tools are your judgment and your willingness to recognize red flags and accept that they are pointing to an avalanche problem. Be humble in the face of natural hazards and you will find that as one door closes another will open, whether it is another route, peak, activity, or epiphany. Being open to change will help you climb for a long time—which is the point, after all!

ABOUT THE AUTHOR: *Based in Seattle, Matt Schonwald is founder of BC Adventure Guides. He is a certified ski mountaineering guide, a certified instructor with the American Avalanche Association, and a member of the Northwest Avalanche Center Forecast team.*

ICE CLIMBERS AND AVALANCHES
IT'S TIME TO TAKE THIS RISK MORE SERIOUSLY

By Grant Statham

Every winter, ice climbers are caught and sometimes killed by avalanches. Even small avalanches can be deadly when they get funneled into the narrow gullies where ice climbs form. So understanding the avalanche conditions and carrying rescue gear when climbing is essential for many climbs.

Yet despite this reality, climbers have been slow to embrace basic avalanche safety practices, even when they always use avalanche gear when backcountry skiing. This contradiction makes no sense, and it's high time for a paradigm shift.

Once you've determined if your ice route is formed, your next move should be to figure out whether it's threatened by avalanches. Any steep snow slopes on the approach, the route, above the route, or on the descent have the potential to release an avalanche.

If your route is threatened by avalanches, then you need to know more. Is the climb located in a gully with avalanche start zones overhead? Will you be climbing through snow slopes above cliffs? How about the approach—will you be walking under avalanche paths or kicking steps up a 40° slope to reach the base? How hard is the route—can you climb fast or will you be exposed to avalanches for hours? What does the local avalanche forecast say? You need to answer all of these questions before going climbing.

Avalanche over the clasic Polar Circus ice route in Canada. See also the cover photo of this edition! *Max Darrah*

AVALANCHE RISK

Avalanche risk in ice climbing has three main ingredients: 1) enough snow to produce an avalanche, 2) avalanche-prone terrain, and 3) climbers exposed to this hazard. Remove any one of these elements and you've eliminated the avalanche risk.

But while eliminating avalanche risk ensures safety, it won't get you up the routes on your hit list that are subject to avalanche hazard. For this, you'll need to manage the risk by assessing its individual elements and understanding how they affect you and your partner.

SNOW

The best indicator of unstable snow is avalanche activity. Both slab avalanches and sluffs are threats to ice climbers, because it doesn't take much to knock you off your front points. If avalanches are occurring near your route, then it's safe to assume the snow on your route is also unstable. Here are the big three factors:

(1) **Precipitation** – new snow and especially rain can overload the snowpack
(2) **Wind** – can move snow at 10 times the snowfall rate and create locally deep slabs
(3) **Temperature** – warming trends, inversions, and temps over 0°C (32°F) produce avalanches

TERRAIN

Minimize your exposure by positioning belays out of avalanche terrain or in protected locations, moving together when you can, moving one at a time when necessary, belaying across exposed slopes, and spending no unnecessary time exposed to avalanches. These are the strategies that keep experienced climbers alive. Here are the terrain basics to keep front of mind:

(1) **Slope angle** – the prime angle for slab avalanches is 30° to 45°
(2) **Aspect** – there are big differences between routes in the shade and in the sun
(3) **Elevation** – snow depth increases with elevation, so be aware of conditions overhead
(4) **Terrain traps** – ice climbs are often in or above terrain features that increase consequences (cliffs, gullies, creeks, etc.)

PEOPLE

For risk to exist, something must be "at risk," and in climbing this is people, deliberately exposing themselves to avalanche hazard. All people are fallible, and human factors are well-recognized as a major contributor to avalanche accidents. Here are some considerations:

(1) **Partners** – climb with people you trust and who share your values around risk
(2) **Decision-making** – trust your instincts and bail if it doesn't feel right
(3) **Trophy hunting** – don't obsess over one climb; have options and let the conditions determine your route
(4) **Group size and speed** – keep your team small and move efficiently

PUBLIC AVALANCHE FORECASTS

An excellent source of information on local conditions is the public avalanche forecast, found at *avalanche.ca* in Canada and *avalanche.org* in the USA. Locals watch the forecast regularly to stay abreast of conditions; start checking it early to get a sense of the snowpack.

Don't climb in avalanche terrain unless the danger rating is *Low* or *Moderate*. When it's *Considerable*, avalanches are likely, so now you need to know specific details about the route and what might trigger an avalanche there. If you don't understand this, then don't climb there. *High* and *Extreme* are obvious—stay out of avalanche terrain.

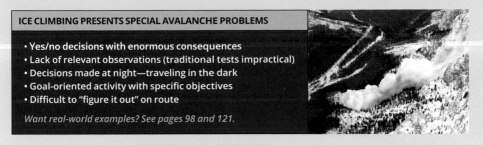

NATURAL RELEASES AND CLIMBER TRIGGERED AVALANCHES

Many ice climbs form directly beneath large avalanche slopes. To climb these routes, you need to determine whether a natural avalanche will release while you're there. This is difficult, but the avalanche forecast, weather forecast, and ridge-top weather stations (accessible online) will provide some of the information you need. Always remember that snow depth, wind effect, and air temperature will be much different high above your climb, so don't be lulled into complacency by snow conditions near your route.

Climbing steep snow is usually part of ice climbing, and this can lead to triggering a slope yourself. Whenever possible, go around snow slopes or cross them as high as you can to reduce the amount of snow above you. If you have to climb directly up the middle of a big slope, the best tactic is to evaluate smaller, safer slopes of similar character to get sense of conditions. Then consider spacing out, going one at a time, or belaying, even if the slope is small but the consequences are catastrophic.

CARRY AVALANCHE RESCUE GEAR

If you're climbing and exposed to avalanche risk, then you should use avalanche rescue gear. If someone gets buried, you have about ten minutes to find them, dig them out, and clear their airway before they asphyxiate. Each member of the team should carry an avalanche transceiver, probe, and shovel. Nobody likes extra weight, so be thoughtful about when and where you carry the gear—plan it out like you plan your rack. Do you only need it for the approach or for the whole route? Maybe take one shovel up the route instead of two. What about the descent?

Even if you're climbing a route where you think an avalanche would be unsurvivable, somebody will still want you back, which means SAR teams will be searching for you. Wearing a transceiver and using clothing equipped with the Recco system does everyone a favor by making you searchable.

RISK AND REWARD

Good avalanche skills are part of being a solid alpinist and waterfall ice climber. While climbing a great route feels awesome, climbing it in good style and doing everything you can to reduce your risk feels even better. Adding risk without additional benefit is pointless, so learn about avalanches, carry the gear, and respond to the ever-changing conditions.

ABOUT THE AUTHOR: *Grant Statham is an ice climber, IFMGA mountain guide, and avalanche forecaster based in Canmore, Alberta. He works with Parks Canada's search and rescue and avalanche safety programs in Banff, Yoho, and Kootenay national parks.*

The mid-elevation area of the West Buttress route on Denali, showing (A) Windy Corner, (B) 14,200-foot camp, (C) headwall with fixed ropes leading to the upper West Buttress, and (D) Denali Pass. Summit is off-picture to the right. *Jeff Plueger*

ALASKA

STRANDED | Extended Storm
Denali, Kahiltna Base Camp

In early March, a team of two climbers (male, 48, and female, 36) returned to Kahiltna base camp at the conclusion of a winter expedition on the West Buttress. They had left a five-day cache of food at base camp, but when a large weather system moved over the Alaska Range, they were unable to fly out as planned. They were in camp for a total of eight and a half days, the last three and a half days without food. After they notified their air taxi service of their situation and requested assistance, the NPS prepared multiple contingencies to rescue these climbers by air or ground. However, a predicted break in the weather on day eight of the storm allowed the air taxi service to retrieve the team.

ANALYSIS

This incident shows that even when prepared for the perceived worst case, a more severe scenario may unfold. These climbers had made conservative risk management decisions during their ascent and descent, in addition to having a contingency cache of food and supplies at base camp. While it might seem unnecessary to plan for an eight- to 10-day storm, every climbing season in the Alaska Range seems to bring such extended storms, which trap climbers along various routes. The more teams prepare in advance, the more comfortable and survivable these long storm cycles will be. (*Source: Denali Mountaineering Rangers.*)

CREVASSE FALL | Snowboarding, Unable to Self-Arrest
Denali, West Buttress

On May 8, a 42-year-old male climber fell while descending on a snowboard at Windy Corner (approximately 13,500 feet). The climber lost an edge while traversing, fell, and was unable to arrest his slide before dropping into a large open crevasse. The climber fractured multiple ribs when he landed at the bottom. The party was unable to self-rescue due to the significant pain from the climber's injuries. His climbing partner alerted the NPS rangers in Talkeetna of the incident, requested assistance, and was in regular contact throughout this extended rescue. The climbers were able to set up camp inside the crevasse, and due to adverse weather and winds at the location, they were forced to shelter there for five days until NPS personnel were able to reach them via ground and air. Ultimately, the climber and partner were rescued via helicopter short-haul.

ANALYSIS
Denali provides the unusual—and often dreaded—opportunity to ski or snowboard downhill while roped and with heavy loads. These skills are often new to climbers, and extreme care should be taken—many expeditions and climbing seasons have ended due to injuries sustained during these activities. Consider double-carrying equipment down through zones with high fall likelihood or descending on foot through these sections. (*Source: Denali Mountaineering Rangers.*)

FALL AT BERGSCHRUND | Inexperience
Denali, West Buttress

On May 10, a 65-year-old male climber injured both knees (injury details unknown) during a fall at 15,200 feet on the West Buttress route. He was attempting to surmount the bergschrund at the base of the fixed lines on this steep section of the route when he fell. This climber was alone, but he was able to crawl down to 14,200-foot camp and notify NPS personnel by radio of his need for a rescue. The climber also developed frostbite injuries to his fingers during the crawl back to camp. Another climbing team in camp assisted the injured climber until he could be flown off the mountain three days later when the weather cleared.

ANALYSIS
The bergschrund at the base of the headwall leading from 14,200-foot camp to the crest of the West Buttress can be a substantial obstacle, especially while carrying a heavy pack. This early season climber was clipped to a fixed line but still fell hard enough to injure his knees. Although he was able to self-rescue to the camp 1,000 feet below the scene of his accident, he required other climbers to care for his injuries while awaiting rescue. The need for conservative decision-making and self-reliance when climbing alone cannot be overstated. (*Source: Denali Mountaineering Rangers.*)

SKIING FALL
Denali, West Buttress

On May 20, a 24-year-old male climber fell while skiing above 14,200-foot camp. The skier was assessed and treated for a suspected dislocated right hip by NPS rescuers and then transported in a rescue toboggan back to camp. After further assessment and with consultation, NPS rangers determined this climber should be flown to definitive care for reduction of a likely dislocation.

ANALYSIS

Extremely varied snow conditions exist in the Alaska Range. This is especially true at higher elevations, due to the greater effect of wind and other weather. Skiers and snowboarders should ride defensively at all times. This skier was fortunate in that he was relatively close to a camp with rescue personnel and because flyable weather allowed for efficient helicopter evacuation. If those two factors had not been in his favor, an extended time period with a dislocated hip could have had a vastly different outcome. (*Source: Denali Mountaineering Rangers.*)

SKIING ON DENALI: *The 2019 Annual Mountaineering Summary for Denali noted a "disturbing trend" of more climbers skiing and snowboarding above 14,200-foot camp on the West Buttress route. "The drastic and variable ski conditions found on the upper mountain are often well above the abilities of the climbers witnessed by the ranger staff," the report said. "There is terrific terrain for skiing on Denali, but that terrain has high— and possibly fatal—consequences. This fact must be considered and prior experience should be gained before skiing/snowboarding during a climbing expedition."*

FROSTBITE

Denali, Upper West Rib

On May 25, a solo 36-year-old male climber was treated for severe frostbite injuries to his fingers and hands. This climber ascended and descended the Upper West Rib climbing route over approximately 22 hours. Upon returning to 14,200-foot camp, he noticed that he had injured his hands and sought assistance. He was assessed by NPS medical personnel and evacuated by air.

ANALYSIS

Frostbite injuries can have long-term consequences. It is critical for climbers to actively rewarm cold body parts before frostbite occurs. When environmental circumstances prevent rewarming, climbers must seek shelter or descend to more hospitable conditions immediately to prevent further injury. [*Editor's Note: These steps are almost always more difficult to accomplish when climbing alone.*] Once frozen body parts are thawed, climbers must prevent refreezing, as that will increase the severity of the original injury. (*Source: Denali Mountaineering Rangers.*)

ANOTHER FROSTBITE INCIDENT: *On June 6, a 47-year-old male climber was evacuated from 17,200-foot camp with deep frostbite to nearly all of his toes and fingers. It is*

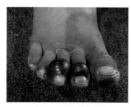

Severe frostbite damage from Denali. *NPS Photo*

not clear if he reached the summit, but he had lost one of his mittens on the upper mountain and wore only a light glove on one hand when his rescue began. This patient had to be lowered from Denali Pass due to the severity of his injuries. A ranger post at the "Denali Dispatches" blog describes the difficulties and teamwork involved in such rescues, as well as some climbers' decisions—including heading for the summit in poor weather—that led to debilitating frostbite injuries during the 2019 season. Search "Denali Lima Charlie" to find the post.

AVALANCHE AND LONG FALL
Kahiltna Queen, West Face

The west face of Kahiltna Queen (a.k.a. Humble Peak). At approximately point X, a skier triggered a small avalanche that caused him to fall to the bottom of the face. *Colin Haley*

On May 28, a 30-year-old male skier fell 700 meters after triggering an avalanche on Kahiltna Queen (a.k.a. Humble Peak). The patient and two companions (all very experienced ski mountaineers) had summited the 12,380-foot peak around noon by the west face, the most commonly climbed route. They reported that the snow "felt safe." They successfully skied the most technical sections without rappels, but as the patient skied the narrows near the top of the route's initial couloir, he triggered a small avalanche and was carried all the way down the 50-degree couloir to the base of the mountain. NPS rescuers responded via air and ground. The rangers suspected injuries to the upper spinal column, and the patient was flown to Talkeetna for further care. Fractures of two cervical vertebrae and multiple ribs were later confirmed.

ANALYSIS

The consequences of climbing or skiing falls in big, remote mountain ranges can be severe. This skier was extremely lucky to have survived this fall. As always, it is paramount to remain vigilant with one's avalanche assessment and safe travel practices. The variable snow conditions and dynamic snow depths found in confined couloirs can cause a skier/snowboarder/climber to trigger an avalanche at a shallow point unknown to the party. This party also reported being hit by a small sluff avalanche while awaiting the rescue. Although injuries may prevent safely moving a patient before a full team of rescuers arrives, the hazards of waiting for help in an exposed location should be weighed. (*Sources: Denali Mountaineering Rangers, patient's report, and the Editors.*)

EXHAUSTION | Inexperience, Inadequate Supplies
Denali, West Buttress

On May 29, a 64-year-old male climber left high camp on the West Buttress for Denali's summit, climbing solo and carrying no food, water, or shelter. During his descent, he was rescued by a guided party and NPS personnel after falling repeatedly on the Autobahn slope, which traverses above 17,200-foot camp to Denali Pass. The NPS team assessed and assisted this climber throughout the remainder of the night, before helping the climber to descend to 14,200-foot camp the next day.

ANALYSIS

This climber was inexperienced and unprepared for the difficulties and hazards of a Denali summit day. In recent years, NPS rangers have witnessed a rise in speed or lightweight summit attempts. Most of these climbers are forgoing valuable supplies in an attempt to move faster. In addition, many seem to be making their decisions to go light to the summit based on the actions of others or due to impending weather, and not based on their own experience or initial planning. When environmental conditions change or a climber's physical state deteriorates on the upper mountain, such climbers are left with little to no margin of safety. Many of these climbers have required assistance or rescue, due to their underestimation of the energy and time required to reach the summit and return safely. (*Source: Denali Mountaineering Rangers.*)

HIGH ALTITUDE PULMONARY EDEMA
Denali, West Buttress

On June 10, a 28-year-old female climber suffering from high altitude pulmonary edema (HAPE) was evacuated by air from 14,200-foot camp. NPS rangers assessed and treated this patient until the helicopter was able to transport her to definitive care at a local hospital.

ANALYSIS
On June 17 and June 22, two other patients were evacuated from 14,200-foot camp with HAPE or acute mountain sickness (AMS). All of these climbers had just arrived at this camp or had done a single acclimatization hike above camp. For many climbers, the low barometric pressure on Denali due to its high latitude makes the altitude feel 2,000 to 3,000 feet higher than the elevation shown on the map. Rarely does severe high-altitude illness present without prior warning lower on the mountain. Continuing to ascend in the midst of even mild altitude illness almost guarantees a worsening illness. AMS typically resolves by remaining at the current elevation for a day or two. Immediate descent is mandatory for all patients suffering from a severe altitude illness. (*Source: Denali Mountaineering Rangers.*)

HIGH ALTITUDE CEREBRAL EDEMA
Denali, West Buttress

On June 14, a 51-year-old male climber and his two climbing partners left late in the afternoon for a summit attempt from 17,200-foot camp. When one of the climbers began to exhibit signs of severe altitude sickness, the group decided to separate, with one of the climbers continuing up and the other accompanying the ill climber back toward high camp. During the descent, the stricken climber became nauseated and began to have difficulty walking. Another climbing team helped guide the patient back to high camp at 17,200 feet. This climbing team was in regular contact with the NPS rangers at 14,200-foot camp and selflessly took care of the patient in their own tent for the next 18 hours. Once weather allowed NPS rescuers to ascend to high camp, they evaluated the patient, confirmed a diagnosis of high altitude cerebral edema (HACE), and called for a helicopter evacuation.

ANALYSIS
This case highlights the benefits of immediate descent for patients exhibiting signs and symptoms of HAPE or HACE. A decrease in altitude often outweighs other medi-

2019 MISLOW-SWANSON DENALI PRO AWARD

The Denali mountaineering rangers selected Ibrahim Cetindemir and Thomas Karst as recipients of the 2019 Mislow-Swanson Denali Pro Award for coming to the aid of a climber stricken with high altitude cerebral edema above Denali Pass. From the award citation: "Embodying the true spirit of this annual award, Cetindemir and Karst abandoned their summit attempt in order to rescue a fellow climber in distress. This honor was created in 1998 to recognize extraordinary actions such as theirs.... Without a doubt, their selfless actions saved the life of a fellow climber."

cal treatments that can be provided for patients at a higher altitude. This party separated, leaving an ill climber with fewer resources and assistance to make it down to high camp. Fortunately, the two other climbers were willing to abandon their own summit attempt and come to this climber's aid. (*Source: Denali Mountaineering Rangers.*)

FALL IN CAMP
Denali, West Buttress

On June 17, a guided 26-year-old female climber injured her right knee after slipping and falling on icy snow in the group's kitchen tent. This climber had injured this knee previously, and an assessment by NPS medical providers confirmed her knee was unusable because of the injury. Without the possibility of bearing weight, the patient was evacuated to Talkeetna by helicopter from 11,200-foot camp.

ANALYSIS
The NPS rangers see a handful of expeditions each season cut short due to injuries that occur during the non-climbing moments of a trip. This accident highlights the need for safe footwear and solid footwork, regardless of the activity. (*Source: Denali Mountaineering Rangers.*)

DANGEROUS BOOTIES: *This climber reportedly was wearing "camp shoes" when she slipped on the icy snow. Most Denali climbers wear various styles of warm booties while resting in camp. In 1993, a climber low on the West Buttress route slipped while descending icy steps into the team's cooking area while wearing down booties and injured his ankle. In 1977, a climber on Mt. Rainier slipped in his booties at camp and fell about 2,000 feet, sustaining serious injuries. Some booties have soles with good traction, but if not they should be improved by gluing carpet scraps or other traction to the soles.*

LOST ON GLACIAL APPROACH
Alaska Range, Hidden Glacier

In mid-June, a team made up of a 30-year-old male and a 37-year-old male attempted to climb Denali's West Buttress from Anchorage; they planned to run and hike to the mountain and then start climbing. Near the Hidden Glacier, south of the head of the Pika Glacier, they realized they would run out of food at their current pace and decided to drop weight and race to a cache they had placed on the Pika Glacier. On June 17, they called to report they were lost and had run out of food, and they requested help. Searchers were unable to find them that day, in part because the "ping" from their satellite phone placed them 10 miles north of their actual location. They were finally located and rescued on June 18 after multiple search attempts by air taxi services and NPS personnel.

ANALYSIS
All routes in the Alaska Range require baseline backcountry skills such as navigation, weather reading, and wilderness survival. The NPS rangers recommend that any climber traveling to the range be as well practiced in these foundational skills as they are in the more technical aspects of a climbing expedition. (*Source: Denali Mountaineering Rangers.*)

HIGH ALTITUDE PULMONARY EDEMA
Denali, West Buttress

Late in the evening on June 22, a team of five climbers began calling for help over the radio. This team had ascended to the Football Field at 19,500 feet on the West Buttress when one of their teammates became ill. The sick climber, a 67-year-old male, seemed unable to descend. With medical guidance over the radio from NPS rangers and help from a guided group in the vicinity, the group was able to slowly descend. The patient was helped down from Denali Pass to 17,200-foot camp by NPS rescuers and then treated in high camp throughout the night for symptoms of HAPE. With minimal improvement by morning, a call was made to evacuate this patient by helicopter for further care.

ANALYSIS
It's fortunate that this climber's team, other climbers in the area, and rangers were able to assist the climber down to high camp, as helicopter rescues at the elevation of the Football Field are rare. (*Source: Denali Mountaineering Rangers.*)

EDITOR'S NOTE: *For the second season in a row, there were no climbing-related fatalities from accidents or illnesses in Denali National Park.*

RAPPEL ANCHOR FAILURE
Juneau Icefield, Mendenhall Towers

A party of three experienced climbers (male, ages 23 to 25) planned to attempt the southeast ridge of the Main Tower in the Mendenhall Towers. The party arrived in the early evening of June 26 by helicopter, set up base camp, and prepared for an alpine start the next morning.

All three had previous experience in the Mendenhall Towers. Two of the three had previously climbed Main Tower, by different routes, and Climbers 1 and 2 had attempted the southeast ridge of the Main Tower in September 2018. This attempt was stopped short after about 1,000 feet of climbing when a loose rock caused a laceration on Climber 2's pinkie finger that resulted in stitches.

In 2019, the party of three left base camp at 6:30 a.m. and, after a long day of swapping leads, they summited around 10:30 p.m. In high spirits they enjoyed the sunset over the Juneau Icefield and began their descent around 11 p.m.

The climbers descended via the ascent route. The nature of the southeast ridge made for numerous short rappels. Old tat, wires, and slung horns were found throughout the descent and used as rappel anchors. The climbers added or replaced these anchors when needed; however, they did not back up the anchors with removable protection while the first and second climber were rappelling. Climber 1 led the rappels throughout the night because he had previous experience with the descent.

After eight to ten rappels (about 1,000 feet), they arrived on a spacious 15- by 20-foot ledge at 1:30 a.m. Each climber was fatigued, dehydrated, and lacking nutrition. However, with base camp now in view, they were motivated to keep going.

The rappel anchor at the large ledge was one bomber large hex and one medium wire, poorly equalized with a cord and a quick-link at the masterpoint. A visual inspection revealed that one end of the cord was frayed and without much space between the knot and the fraying end; Climber 1 also noted the anchor cord was the same as he had seen on this anchor the year prior. After a short discussion, the climbers concluded the anchor was good enough. The party began rappelling without replacing the cord or backing up the anchor.

Climber 1 started down, and in an effort to save time he bypassed the next spacious ledge, about 40 feet below, and continued down the ridge on rappel to a small ledge, descending a total of about 100 feet. He found a suitable horn to sling and went off rappel. Climber 2 rigged his rappel device, walked from the anchor to the lip of the ledge (15 feet), weighted the rope, and instantly the anchor failed. Climber 2 fell to the next ledge 40 feet below, taking the rappel rope with him in his fall. Climber 1, down below, did not witness the fall, only heard a very loud thud. Climber 3 witnessed the anchor failure: Both pieces of rock protection were still in the wall, but the cord that had connected the pieces was at his feet.

Climber 3, perched on the ledge above, was able to see and hear Climber 2 after the fall. He was lying on his side and not responsive, only moaning. Immediately, Climber 3 called 911 and informed dispatch of the severity of the accident and the need for a helicopter; this phone call took place around 1:45 a.m. Climber 1 and Climber 3 both carried cell phones, and Climber 1 was able to use GPS services from the phone

Southeast buttress of Main Tower in the Mendenhall Towers. (1) Location of rappel anchor that failed. (2) Ledge where the rappeller landed and eventually was rescued by helicopter.

to relay their location to 911 and the Coast Guard. A Coast Guard helicopter was dispatched from Sitka shortly after 2:30 a.m. with an ETA of one and half hours to Juneau, followed by a short flight to the Mendenhall Towers.

The accident had left Climber 3 without a rope or gear to descend to Climber 2's position 40 feet below. Climber 1 was about 70 feet lower and held the ends of the rappel rope, but since the rope was no longer anchored, he could not ascend it. As they waited for help, Climber 3 continued to monitor Climber 2 from above, and around 3:30 a.m., in the first light of the morning, he was able to communicate directly with Climber 1. He relayed that Climber 2 was not moving and that blood had flowed from the back of his head. Climber 1 decided to climb up to Climber 2, whom he reached around 4 a.m. He noticed minor sounds of moaning and a light pulse from climber 2's radial artery.

Shortly before 4:12 a.m., the Coast Guard helicopter arrived. The climbers used the red flashing mode on their headlamps to signal the helicopter. (A crew member later said the red flashes were very helpful in pinpointing their location on the large, dark wall.) Climber 1 prepared Climber 2 for the helicopter by cutting his rappel device from the rope and untangling the rope. Climber 1 noticed the quick-link from the failed rappel anchor was still connected to the rope. At 4:30 a.m., the Coast Guard rescuers efficiently plucked Climber 2 off the mountain and flew him to Bartlett Regional Hospital in Juneau.

Back on the wall, Climber 1 was able to throw some gear up to Climber 3 so he could rig a rappel. Both climbers then rappelled safely down the rest of the route and returned to their base camp at 8 a.m. They flew back to town by helicopter, arriving at 10 a.m., and joined Climber 2 at the hospital. Sadly, the injuries the climber sustained were not survivable, and he died at 11:27 a.m. on June 28.

ANALYSIS

The party's decision not to replace the old tat on the rappel anchor proved to be a fatal mistake. This decision was made in a very fatigued state, and the climbers' judgments were impaired. They prioritized getting back to base camp quickly over taking extra time to ensure the safety of their anchors. This seems like a very misguided error, but in the early hours of the morning, running on little sleep, dehydrated and hungry, you may make odd decisions you would not otherwise.

In addition to replacing or supplementing the old tat on the anchor, the climbers could have backed up each of their anchors while the first two climbers were rappelling. The third and lightest person to rappel could have removed the backups before starting down.

Complacency in the face of risk led the climbers to decide the rappel anchor was good enough. These climbers were young and had had an abundance of positive experiences in climbing. They had completed more then half of the rappels already. They let their guard down too early. (*Source: Climber 1.*)

BRYSON ALLEN WILDERNESS EXPERIENCE FUND: *Friends and family of Bryson Allen (Climber 2) have established a scholarship fund for incoming University of Montana students who might otherwise not be able to participate in the annual Freshman Wilderness Experience. Info at umt.edu/crec/about/support/bryson-allen-fund.php.*

ARIZONA

RAPPEL ERROR | Used Wrong Strand of Rope
Sycamore Canyon, Paradise Forks

On May 5, a climber (24) took a 20-foot ground fall after attempting a fixed-line rappel to the base of a cliff at Paradise Forks. While it is not known what knot or block was being used at the anchor, rescuers report the climber attached her rappel device to a short tail of rope rather than the full fixed line. When she weighted her system, she fell. The climber suffered unspecified leg injuries.

ANALYSIS
The fall was a result of not double-checking the rappel setup and not testing it prior to committing to the rappel. Always weight-test the rope while you're still clipped into the anchor. Even very experienced climbers make mistakes when setting up rappels—safety checks are for everyone. (*Source: Paul Clifton, Coconino County Search and Rescue.*)

GROUND FALL | Inexperience, Inadequate Belay
The Pit, Mall Wall

On October 28, Zachary Dreher (23) had just passed the last bolt on Bluto Tastes an Olive (5.10a sport) when he fell. His belayer (female, 22) lost control of the belay, and Zachary took a 38-foot ground fall. The belayer was using an ATC-style device. The belayer had rope burns on her right hand, and Zachary suffered a broken right pelvis and fractured L1 vertebra. He was not wearing a helmet.

ANALYSIS
Zachary stated that his partner was very inexperienced and he should have done more instruction before allowing her to belay on her own. Whenever teaching someone to belay, it is a good idea to have another climber act as a backup belayer, holding the brake strand of the rope behind the belayer and reinforcing essential techniques, such as the importance of always maintaining a hand on the brake strand. According to the Coconino County Sheriff's Office, the climber weighed approximately twice as much as the belayer, and she was pulled off her feet before losing control of the rope. (*Sources: Zachary Dreher, Coconino County Sheriff's Office, and the Editors.*)

GROUND FALL | Scrambling Toward Rappel Anchors
Mt. Lemmon, Chimney Rock, Standard Route

At approximately 10:30 a.m. on April 12, my brother-in-law, Stephen Whittingham, and I (Chris, 30) were at the top of the Standard Route (5.7) on Chimney Rock, preparing to descend. The rappel anchor was on the far east end of the summit, out of range of the small tree we used for an anchor at the top of our climb. I unclipped from our

Site of the fall at the top of Chimney Rock. *Stephen Whittingham*

anchor, grabbed the two ends of the rope, and started moving across the summit toward the rap anchor. That's the last thing I remember before I fell.

As told by Stephen: Out of my peripheral vision I could see Chris take a leaping step in the direction of the rappel anchors. Either his momentum was too great or the ledge he anticipated landing on didn't exist because, with a scream that I will never forget, he fell 30 feet, out of my sight. I took the phone from my pocket to dial 911. I remained on the line with dispatch for a total of 46 minutes. I consciously made the decision to stay at the top after calling 911, because I believed it was most important for me to have a view of the road and direct responders to Chris' position. I am an engineer and don't have any experience related to emergency medicine.

From one vantage point, I could see Chris at the base of the rock, and at first he appeared to be unconscious but soon began to stir.

As an ambulance came up the mountain, I took a couple of bright climbing slings off my shoulder and began waving them around my head. When the ambulance got closer, the driver honked, signaling that he saw me. A sheriff's deputy arrived, and I tried to yell down the best way for someone to reach Chris' location.

Sometime after noon, I could hear the unmistakable chop of an approaching helicopter. Again, I took the climbing slings from my chest and swung them around my head to capture the pilot's attention, then pointed to the side of the rock where Chris was lying. Soon after, a rescuer was being lowered to the ground. I now made my way over to the rappel station and flaked out my rope for a rappel. Back on the ground, I assisted in placing a neck brace and positioning Chris on a backboard. The deputy maneuvered him into a hoist bag. In mere seconds, Chris was at the helicopter and was flown down the mountain to an awaiting ambulance. I remember looking down at my watch and the time was 12:43 p.m., about two hours after the accident.

As told by Chris: I had a concussion and a number of broken bones in my face but did not have any head bleed or skull fracture. Somehow, both my nose and jaw escaped unharmed, although my lip and left ear had some pretty severe lacerations, and two bones in my right ankle were broken. (*Sources: Chris Czaplicki and Stephen Whittingham.*)

ANALYSIS

Like most accidents in climbing, this one was preventable. Although it was not possible to reach the rappel anchor from the anchor I built off the small tree, I could have made the decision to extend it with one or two of the many slings I had with me. Large ledges or summits may provide a false sense of security, and I hope this write-up encourages readers to stay on anchor or build a new anchor while maneuvering across an uneven ledge with potentially deadly exposure. [*Editor's Note: Another good option is to maintain a belay while each climber makes the transition between anchors.*]

Another lesson I learned from this is the importance of having a means to call for a rescue. While I had a personal locator beacon with me, it was down in my pack at the base of the climb. Thankfully, Stephen had brought his cellphone and we had service. (*Source: Chris Czaplicki.*)

CALIFORNIA

MT. SHASTA ANNUAL SUMMARY
Mt. Shasta and Castle Crags Wilderness

In 2019 there were 16 climbing-related incidents on Mt. Shasta. Twelve accidents were due to falls on ice or snow, and four climbers attempting the summit became lost. This is the second year of above-average rescues on Mt. Shasta, and one accident resulted in a fatality.

On May 11, a 53-year-old male climber who had separated from his party fell at the Heart (12,300 feet), was unable to self-arrest, and tumbled approximately 1,000 feet. His fall was slowed and eventually stopped by two climbers who "jumped on him" as he slid in the Upper Moraine. He suffered facial trauma, a left shoulder/arm injury, and a traumatic brain injury (TBI). Other climbers built a platform and secured the patient to the slope with an ice axe anchor. As responders prepared the patient for evacuation, two of the climbers moved upslope with their shovels to deflect falling rime ice, which was greater than normal and a real objective hazard. The climber was evacuated by helicopter.

On June 2, a female climber, age 23, slipped while skinning toward Helen Lake, falling approximately 500 feet. Mt. Shasta climbing rangers responded to the injured climber and conducted a patient assessment that revealed a femur fracture. They constructed a snow platform and attempted to apply a makeshift traction device until a California Highway Patrol (CHP) helicopter arrived to evacuate the injured climber. On June 8, a male, age 39, fell while skiing in Avalanche Gulch and slid 600 feet, suffering probable broken ribs. He too was evacuated by helicopter. Both skiers' falls happened on days when the snow was very smooth and icy.

On June 9, three separate accidents occurred on Shasta. The first, at 5:50 a.m., happened when a 60-year-old male slipped in Avalanche Gulch and fell headfirst for 800 feet until stopped by two climbers. The climber was unconscious for five minutes and suffered a TBI and facial trauma. Later in the morning, a climber slipped and fell on the west face route. Little is known about how this accident occurred, but the climber suffered minor abrasions and an unknown leg injury. The final accident of the day occurred in Avalanche Gulch at 1 p.m. when a 49-year-old male fell while descending and suffered abrasions and lacerations to his lower back, lower chest, and arms.

On June 14, a male climber, age 76, slipped and fell on the Avalanche Gulch route. The accident occurred when the climber saw one of his partner's crampons come loose and attempted to stop the crampon from sliding down the hill. The climber lost his ice axe and slid 300 feet before hitting a large ice block. He suffered a fractured thumb, a minor neck fracture, rib fracture, and large leg contusion. The climber was hoisted and evacuated by helicopter.

On August 14, two climbers summited Mt. Shasta via the Clear Creek Route. This was the conclusion of an extended hiking trip that began in Ashland, Oregon, and traversed seven wilderness areas. Reaching the summit late in the day, the

The Whitney Glacier on the north side of Mt. Shasta. The circle marks the crevasse that two under-equipped climbers/hikers slid into during an attempted glissade. *Nick Meyers | USFS*

pair decided to bivy near the top. The next morning the party mistakenly descended the Whitney Glacier rather than their intended route down the west face. They did not have ice axes, crampons, helmets, or other mountaineering gear—only running shoes with short gaiters for footwear. The two decided they would try to glissade down the head of the Whitney Glacier. The two began their glissade together, with the female climber hugging her boyfriend from behind. They quickly lost control, sliding directly into a bergschrund at approximately 13,000 feet.

The male climber landed face-first on the downhill side of the bergschrund, breaking his sunglasses on the firm snow and ice, but was otherwise uninjured. The female climber landed directly on top of him and then fell back into the bergschrund, landing about 25 feet down. Fortunately, she was able to catch herself on a small ice shelf but was unable to climb out. Miraculously, good cell service inside the crevasse allowed a 911 call. Siskiyou County SAR and USFS rangers responded immediately and inserted ranger Nick Meyers to the scene. He constructed a snow anchor and lowered a rope to the injured climber. After conducting a quick verbal assessment of her injuries and instructing her on how to secure herself to the rope, ranger Meyers and the boyfriend manually hoisted her to the surface as she stemmed up the sides of the crevasse. The injured climber was evacuated by helicopter hoist; she had suffered minor cuts and bruises, and was very cold and humbled.

The very next day, August 15, a 30-year-old male climber fell while attempting a one-day climb of the Avalanche Gulch route. He and his partner were equipped with lightweight distance-running-style backpacks, Gore-tex running shoes, microspikes instead of crampons, and ice axes. The team got off route above Helen Lake, moving right onto the flank of Sargents Ridge, a steep snow slope known locally as the Alaska Chute. About halfway up, the climber attempted to adjust his microspikes as they were beginning to come off. He slipped while doing so and fell several hundred feet, hitting a rock and severely injuring his right ankle. Rangers lowered the patient by SKED to the upper moraine above Helen Lake, from which he was evacuated by helicopter.

The final accident of the 2019 climbing season on Mt. Shasta, on August 31, resulted in a fatality when a 27-year-old male slipped and fell while descending in Avalanche Gulch. The climber was a member of a larger party that was off-route (far climber's left) on the slope of Casaval Ridge. An older member of the team had slipped, injuring his leg and face, and the team had decided to descend rather than continue up the mountain. They prepared to use a rope to lower the injured climber. At this point, the 27-year-old decided to descend by himself without using the rope. What exactly occurred at this point is unknown, as the fall was unobserved, but the team later found the climber unconscious, with head injuries and facial trauma. A local paramedic and flight crew member who was climbing at the time, Scott Half-erman, came to the immediate aid of the climber, along with rangers and members of the CHP helicopter crew. Unfortunately, the climber succumbed to his injuries on September 2.

ANALYSIS
Search and rescue incidents on Mt. Shasta were elevated for the second year in a row, even as the number of summit passes remained only slightly above the yearly average of passes since 1997. Winter and spring storms resulted in heavy snowpack on the mountain, but late storms (into May) did little to discourage climbers. As in previous years, falls on steep snow and failure to self-arrest were the primary cause for injury.

Rangers at Mt. Shasta continually focus their education efforts on the importance of self-arrest, navigation in mountainous terrain, proper preparation (skills, ability, and equipment), and how to plan for self-rescue. These skills and having situational awareness are keys to a successful summit and descent. (*Source: Mt. Shasta and Castle Crags Wilderness 2019 Climbing Ranger Report and Search and Rescue Incident Narratives.*)

LEAD FALL ONTO LEDGE | Protection Pulled Out
Donner Summit, Black Wall

Late on July 12, two male climbers were attempting to complete the second pitch of Cannibal Gully, a 5.7 trad climb on the left portion of the Black Wall. This climb is popular for new leaders due to the grade, but the rock quality is considered low for the area. The leader fell at approximately 25 feet above a large ledge. An unknown number of pieces blew, causing him to hit the ledge, bounce, and continue falling for another ten feet before being stopped by his belayer. The climber, who was severely injured, was unable to climb back to the belay, so the belayer tied off his injured partner and called for assistance.

Members of Truckee Tahoe Regional Rescue Team responded to the top of the wall and lowered a rescuer with a Stokes basket, secured the injured climber, and assisted the party to the bottom of the cliff. The leader suffered numerous traumatic injuries, including a fractured pelvis, fractured back, and a head injury. He was wearing a helmet. (*Source: Dave Fichter, Truckee Tahoe Regional Rescue Team.*)

ANALYSIS
This climb, established in 1969, is an "old school" 5.7, and many climbers feel that it is much harder than the grade suggests, compared with today's standards. Many new trad leaders are drawn to its low grade and easy appearance, but the rock quality of this climb is poor and a number of accidents have occurred here over the years. [*A second accident occurred on this climb on August 16 when a leader (male, age unknown) fell after getting his foot stuck in the crack. He suffered a fractured ankle.*] Whatever a climber's experience level, placing ample protection on traditional routes is a must. When encountering suspect rock, additional protection can help to prevent a long fall should one of the pieces fail. (*Sources: Dave Fichter, Truckee Tahoe Regional Rescue Team and the Editors.*)

FALL WHILE TOPPING OUT | No Spotter
Tahoe, Eagle Falls, Lost in Space Boulders

On May 5, a boulderer (male, 32), fell while topping out an unnamed V4 near the south shore of Lake Tahoe. He fell about ten feet, landing awkwardly onto his pad. He was climbing with friends but had no spotter at the time. Upon landing, he sustained a severe open fracture ankle dislocation. Two friends came to his assistance and contacted El Dorado Search and Rescue. Due to snow conditions and the severity of the fracture, the climber was airlifted by California Highway Patrol (CHP) to a local hospital, where he underwent emergency surgery to repair the ankle.

ANALYSIS
This accident occurred within a mile of the highway but across a river and in heavy spring snow conditions, making self-rescue impossible. Fortunately, the friends who were bouldering nearby were able to contact search and rescue, and air evacuation was completed just prior to sunset. Due to the nature of the fracture, any additional delay could have significantly affected the prospects for recovery. The climber believes this accident would have been prevented if he'd had a spotter to guide his landing. No matter how easy a problem is, it's always best to have spotters. (*Source: Carolina Rodríguez, friend of the injured climber.*)

A NOTE ON BOULDERING ACCIDENTS: *This bouldering incident was unusual because it led to a rescue involving a helicopter and other significant resources. Accidents in North American Climbing reports few bouldering incidents, but not because they are rare—we see anecdotal reports about numerous injuries, usually involving the lower legs. However, most boulderers who get hurt rely on their friends and other climbers to self-rescue and get medical attention, and thus the accidents are never reported officially. Good spotting, the careful placement of pads, and appropriate choice of problems for one's skill and experience will prevent many bouldering accidents.*

LEADER FALL ONTO LEDGE | Off-Route, Inadequate Protection
Lake Tahoe Area, Sugarloaf

On August 3, I (female, 20) was leading Scheister, a three-pitch 5.7 trad route at Sugarloaf. On the third pitch, I climbed about 25 feet above the belay before realizing I had gone the wrong way. I had only placed one nut, clipped to the rope with a short quickdraw. While downclimbing to correct my mistake, I grabbed the nut and weighted it. It immediately blew out, and I landed on a big ledge about ten feet below. I could tell my right foot was broken; it would not support my weight.

My partner found an anchor using two bolts on a nearby climb and we rappelled to the next bolted anchor and then to the ground. He went first and put me on a fireman's belay each time. I was able to crawl 400 meters down the steep trail to my car and drive home. I had a cuboid bone fracture in my right foot that required surgery.

ANALYSIS
Before I weighted the nut, I noticed that it had moved a little out of its placement, likely due to movement of the rope. A longer sling might have prevented this from

occurring. I gave it a tug and it did not move, so I assumed it would hold my full weight, even though the placement no longer looked perfect. An additional gear placement may have prevented me from hitting the ledge. The whole need to downclimb could have been avoided if I had studied the topo better and found the correct line before climbing. (*Source: Katarina Owens.*)

LEADER FALL ON ALPINE ROCK | Haste, Climber Out of Sight
High Sierra, Incredible Hulk, Red Dihedral

On the morning of September 9, Dan (28) and Jon (30) started up the Red Dihedral route (12 pitches, 5.10) with a party of three climbers close behind. The leader of the first party, Dan, had nearly finished the second pitch when he slipped and fell about 30 feet, despite being only five feet above his last protection. Dan quickly realized that his ankle was severely injured.

After conferring with the party below them, Jon lowered Dan to the ledge where the second team was stationed, approximately ten feet below Jon's belay. The second party had added three pieces of gear and a thicker cordelette to their anchor to accommodate this larger load. Anticipating a potential lower, the second team attached Dan to their anchor with a Munter mule hitch. Dan then untied from his rope so Jon could rappel down to the group.

The Incredible Hulk formation, west of Bridgeport in the Sawtooth Range. The Red Dihedral is near the right edge of the wall, and the climber camps are at the base of the large talus field. *Dan Z.*

The second party had a satellite communication device, and after considering the difficulty of the descent and hike out, which includes third-class terrain, Dan and Jon decided to use the device to call for a rescue.

The group decided to lower Dan and Jon with both parties' ropes tied together. Using a Munter hitch, they first lowered Dan, then pulled the rope back up to lower Jon. They then untied the ropes and tossed Dan and Jon's rope back to them. Though the second party initially intended to keep climbing, they eventually decided to rappel, and they helped Dan and Jon back to their camp at the base of the talus. A California Highway Patrol helicopter transported Dan to the hospital in Mammoth Lakes, where it was confirmed he had fractured his right ankle in two places. (*Sources: Dan and Jon.*)

ANALYSIS
The direct cause of this accident was a fall on less-than-vertical terrain. Especially in remote areas, climb conservatively to avoid falls in terrain where lack of protection or ledges indicate injury potential. Dan acknowledged that this climb was at the top reach of his limits, and because of a biking injury he had sustained two months prior, he had not been climbing much in the lead-up to this trip.

Jon was unable to see Dan when he fell and may have had more slack in the belay system than normal. It can be tricky to manage the rope when the leader is out of sight, and care is required to prevent slack from inadvertently piling on ledges or in cracks.

Dan also indicated that he felt rushed by the second party catching up to them, despite everyone's apparent patience. He was trying to climb quickly to be courteous, when he should have prioritized climbing safely. In popular areas like the Incredible Hulk, finding multiple parties on the same route is common. While it can be frustrating to be stuck behind a slower party, patience and good communication usually will lead to an opportunity for the faster team to pass.

The second party in this incident is to be commended for having the skills to execute an effective self-rescue, having the appropriate communication device to call for assistance, and helping Dan and Jon down the talus. The climbers were fortunate the accident was early in the day, the weather permitted a helicopter to fly, and the second team carried a satellite communication device. (Dan and Jon had a cell phone, but there is no reception in this area.) Without these things, the injured party might have endured a long wait for help. (*Sources: Dan, Jon, Will (member of the second party), and the Editors.*)

FALL ON ROCK | Crowded Climb
Yosemite National Park, Tuolumne Meadows, Cathedral Peak

John and Chris (30-year-old males) were on their first climbing trip to Yosemite, and Cathedral was their first objective. They had climbed together frequently in the past, and had completed a three-day course in multi-pitch trad climbing in 2017. They were comfortable leading 5.8 with traditional gear.

On October 6, they arrived at the base of Cathedral around noon. They could see four or five other parties on the popular southeast buttress: two parties down low and one higher up with three people. At this point, they decided to seek variations that would allow them to avoid other parties. They simul-climbed the first couple of pitches, with John leading the first block and Chris leading the second block, which took them to the level of the chimney about three pitches up.

At this point, one party was in the chimney with another party waiting at its base. Because of the crowds, Chris chose to set up his anchor on the ledge about 30 feet to the left of the chimney and bring John up to there. They planned to pitch out the climbing from this point, since they were entering harder terrain. According to the Supertopo topo they had with them, the climbing to the left of the chimney went at 5.7.

Chris had built his anchor in a left-facing corner, but John opted to climb further left on the face in order to avoid climbing directly through the anchor. As John climbed off the ledge, he got himself into an awkward position that didn't feel like 5.7 climbing, and with his feet approximately six to eight feet off the ledge, he barndoored off. At this point he hadn't placed any gear, and as he began to fall he made the split-second decision to try and land on the ledge rather than push off the wall and risk a factor 2 fall on the anchor.

John landed awkwardly on his feet and stumbled into a sitting position. He immediately knew that he had injured his legs. Continuing up wasn't an option, and though Supertopo showed a bail option off the right side of Cathedral, that would still involve hiking down through unfamiliar terrain. John and Chris decided their best strategy would be to self-rescue to the base and receive further help there.

Chris and John began rapping the route, leaving gear and slinging horns for anchors every 30 meters, since they only had one rope. John used one hand as his brake hand and the other to push himself away from the wall. At 3:23 p.m., he called 911. Ten minutes later, two responders were dispatched on foot from Tuolumne Meadows and a helicopter was ordered.

As Chris was setting up their fourth rappel anchor (approximately 150 feet off the ground), they saw two soloists arrive at the base. The soloists happened to be ex-YOSAR members and medical professionals, and they climbed over to help the pair with patient care and anchor building, and then lowered John down the final pitches with one of the responders, who at that point had arrived on scene.

At the base, John was assessed and splinted, and at 6:13 p.m. he was flown away from the scene by helicopter. He was diagnosed with fractures in both ankles.

ANALYSIS
Right above the ledge where John fell was a finger size crack, which he used for hand holds but not for protection. Placing good gear early when climbing off the ground or above a ledge can often prevent injury in the event of a fall.

The crowding on this very popular route not only adds objective hazards such as rockfall but also changes the entire mindset of parties who are feeling the pressure of crowds. Rather than focusing on climbing the best line, John and Chris opted for less desirable variations and were operating in a hastier mindset, which can affect decision-making and risk analysis. This is not the first accident on this climb where crowds were likely a contributing factor. The rock is not going anywhere—if there are too many people, another route or a different day might be a safer choice.

John and Chris' ability to safely build anchors and rappel most of the route helped immensely to expedite the rescue. However, some skills were rusty, such as how a rescuer can rappel with a patient (tandem rappel), which would have sped their descent and provided better patient care. Learn these skills and then practice them often, before they are needed. (*Source: Yosemite National Park Climbing Rangers.*)

STRANDED | Stuck Rappel Rope
Yosemite Valley, Royal Arches

On June 8, Chad and Ben started up Royal Arches (III 5.7 A0). Both were experienced climbers, with two years of trad experience around the 5.7/5.8 level. The team started climbing around 9 a.m., and they reached the final anchors at 8:45 p.m. They then had the option of descending via the North Dome Gully or the Royal Arches rappel route. The party opted to rappel and began the 18 single-rope rappels to the valley floor.

They were prepared with two headlamps, lightweight jackets, arm warmers, a basic first-aid kit, two cell phones, and six liters of water for the day. At 10:30 p.m., they completed their fifth rappel. However, while pulling the rope,

Knot that formed while pulling a rappel rope, forcing a pair of climbers to spend the night at a six-inch ledge. *NPS Photo* it got stuck at the anchor above them. They now only had one end of the rope, and steep, unprotected slab separated them from the upper anchor. They chose not to climb the unprotected face with the remaining slack or to ascend the rope.

Chad and Ben called for a rescue with one of their phones. Yosemite Search and Rescue was busy on a serious call, so the pair spent the night at the anchor on a six-inch-wide ledge. The following morning, two members of YOSAR climbed Royal Arches and rappelled from above to access the stranded climbers' rope. They discovered a giant slip knot that had formed while the climbers were pulling the rappel rope; the knot had gotten stuck at the rap rings. The rescuers untied the knot, and together the four continued rappelling to the base.

ANALYSIS

Making a long series of rappels late into the night is a nerve-wracking exercise. Improve your odds of smooth pulls by noting where the anchors are located, the terrain where the rope will run, and how the rope is placed through the anchors. Pull the rope slowly in the direction and angle that will yield the cleanest drop. While one person pulls the rope, the other can watch for knots, snarls, or serious twists.

If the rope gets stuck at the anchor above, the climbers must decide whether to ascend the rope, lead back to the anchor using whatever rope and protection are available, continue to descend with whatever rope can be salvaged, or wait for help. Every situation is different, and Chad and Ben were well prepared for the decision they made, with extra layers, headlamps, sufficient water, and cell phones to call for help. (*Source: Yosemite National Park Climbing Rangers and the Editors.*)

LONG LEADER FALL | Protection Failures, Fatigue
Yosemite Valley, El Capitan, Salathé Wall

In mid-June, Rylan Knuttgen and John Shields started up the Salathé Wall. Both were experienced climbers with four decades of trad climbing between them, including multiple big walls. They had been prepping for the Salathé Wall specifically for the last 18 months and felt physically and mentally prepared for the route.

The climb went well until, on June 15, they trended too far right on pitch 26, leading to Sous le Toit ledge from the Block. After encountering tricky aid and loose rock, they realized they were off-route and were able to rappel back to the Block and then continue on the correct line. However, this cost them about seven hours, and they didn't arrive at Long Ledge, their planned bivy site, until 4:30 a.m. on the 16th.

By midmorning they were awake and preparing for the final four pitches of the route. They had received a weather report the previous day calling for a chance of thunderstorms in the afternoon, and they wanted to be off the wall before bad weather arrived.

At this point they had to decide between the original aid route off Long Ledge, which heads up a C2 crack on the far right side, and a free variation that follows bolts up steep rock above the left side. The free variation is given a grade of 5.11d/5.12a, whereas the climbing above the C2 crack is rated 5.8 in the Supertopo guidebook. However, they also had a topo from MountainProject.com that showed "5.10b R polished knobs" on the right-hand line, and they were aware of the notoriety of that pitch. [*Editor's Note: There have been many long falls from this pitch, including ones causing serious injuries.*] When gathering beta for the climb in the Valley beforehand, they had not found anyone who had climbed the left variation, and so were hesitant to go that way, despite their topo suggesting it might be the "best way." After discussing their options, they opted to follow the right-hand line.

John took the lead and was feeling good despite their lack of sleep. At the top of the crack, he found a fixed gray Fixe Alien Revolution that looked to be in good shape, and he clipped it as pro. (He had approximately seven pieces of pro in the crack below that.) Here, the available gear placements start to dwindle and then disappear. Above the fixed piece, John was able to place a black (tiny) Alien, but had very little confidence the piece would hold a fall. John had to switch to free climbing and communicated that to Rylan. He also noted that a piton shown by Supertopo was missing. As John climbed through the polished knobs, he shouted down to Rylan that it would be "a hell of a whipper" if he fell, and as he was readjusting his feet to reach the final jug he slipped.

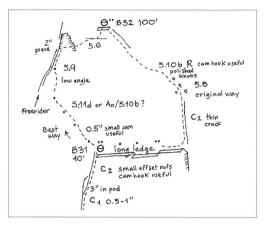

Topo showing two options for the notorious pitch above Long Ledge, high on the Salathé Wall. The best choice will depend on the leader's Yosemite free climbing skills. *Pep Soldevila | Mountain Project*

John fell from approximately 12 feet above his last piece and swung to the right as multiple pieces failed under load. He narrowly missed hitting Long Ledge and ultimately stopped about 20 feet below the ledge, after taking a fall of 50 to 60 feet. He had hit the wall several times on the way down. John immediately recognized he would need a rescue because of injuries (multiple broken bones), but took it upon himself to ascend his rope and get back onto Long Ledge.

Attached to his rope was the black Alien (an expected failure), part of the fixed Alien, which had broken at the stem, and one extra sling that most likely came unclipped from a piece below the Alien. John was most likely caught by a number 1 Black Diamond C4, which was approximately 20 to 25 feet below his fall point.

After a quick assessment, during which they determined John had no head or spine injury, Rylan tried to call 911 multiple times but was unable to get through. Knowing there were parties below them, they started shouting for someone to call for help. A party on Mammoth Terraces (nearly 2,000 feet below) heard them and called 911.

A helicopter was ordered to make contact with the parties, and though unable to communicate verbally, John and Rylan indicated that they needed help by waving. YOSAR team members were flown to the top of El Capitan to launch a top-down extrication of the party, who were about 400 feet below the rim. A rescuer was lowered to the pair and then raised back to the top with John in a litter and then again with Rylan. John was flown from the summit. He sustained multiple injuries to the left side of his body, including a fractured ulna, tibia/fibula, and talus bones.

ANALYSIS

The failure of two or more pieces was a major factor in turning what might have been a long but reasonably safe fall into a very long and damaging fall. Be extremely cautious with fixed gear, which may be significantly damaged or weakened (or poorly placed). There's a chance John could have removed the fixed cam and used his own piece in that placement. It's also possible that a different piece than the black Alien might have caught his fall. Especially with micro-cams, slight variance in size (often necessitating a different brand of protection) can make a huge difference in the piece's holding power. When facing a runout above critical pieces, take the time to be confident of the quality of each gear placement.

After three days on the wall and their late night beforehand, this team was not at their peak climbing shape. They were also feeling the pressure of possible thunderstorms. John and Rylan had enough food and water for extra time on the wall and a fly for their portaledge to wait out a storm. It's possible that if they had rested and recovered, they might have avoided the fall.

These climbers had thoroughly researched their climb by looking at multiple topos and talking to others who had been on the route. Their decision to take the right-hand variation off Long Ledge made sense, given the information they had gathered. However, had they been able to talk with a climber who had done the left-hand variation, which goes with reachy 5.10+ free climbing and aid off bolts, they might have gone that way. (*Source: Yosemite National Park Climbing Rangers.*)

LEAD FALL | Cam Pulled Out
Yosemite Valley, Lower Falls Amphitheater

In late October, I completed a number of routes at Yosemite Falls with some friends. I decided to lead Guiding Light (5.10b trad), a dihedral about 80 feet long with a thinning crack and stemming on slick feet. The line culminates with a thin layback crux about three-quarters of the way up. This route is well within my onsight ability.

Prior to entering the crux, I placed a yellow number 2 Metolius TCU in a flared pin scar at head level. I had a number 6 Black Diamond Stopper roughly a body length below that. I was at a good stance while double-checking the cam placement, and I made sure all three lobes had good contact and were cammed to the green dots on the range finder. With the cam two or three feet below my feet, my right foot smear slipped and I fell. During the fall I may have unknowingly hit and slightly altered the cam placement.

As my rope came taut, I heard a pop and felt the cam impact my right temple, at which time I began to fall again until my next piece (the Stopper) caught me. I suffered a scalp laceration that did not require stitches.

ANALYSIS

I could have "nested" gear due to the marginal placement in a piton scar and connected the pieces with a runner to equalize them. Additionally, I should have been wearing a helmet, as it would have protected me during the fall and from my pulled gear. [*Editor's Note: It's often necessary to "punch it" to a good stance while leading layback cracks, and doubling up on protection is wise before committing to such sequences.*] (*Source: Ryan Wood.*)

FALL ON ROCK
Yosemite Valley, Sentinel Rock, Steck-Salathé Route

In the evening of October 18, Yosemite National Park dispatchers received a report of a fallen climber on the 13th pitch of the Steck-Salathé Route on Sentinel Rock, a prominent Yosemite Valley feature infamous for its demanding wide cracks and arduous approach and descent. Climber 1, an experienced climber in her 30s, was leading when she found herself off-route. Nervous about downclimbing, she climbed to a fixed nut and planned to lower back to the belay. However, when she weighted the nut, it pulled out. She fell approximately 30 feet, hitting her face and resulting in a brief loss of consciousness and several broken teeth.

After the leader regained consciousness, the party of two were unsure if they would be able to continue climbing, and a rescue was initiated. A team of Yosemite Valley rescue personnel hiked up the Sentinel's descent gully. Meanwhile, the party had decided to continue, and they made it to the top of the Sentinel as the rescue team reached them. The injured party was treated and monitored overnight and flown out via helicopter in the morning.

ANALYSIS
It's not uncommon to find oneself off-route on long adventure climbs like the Steck-Salathé. The party in this incident were climbing within their skill set but made a significant error: trusting fixed gear. Yosemite Valley is full of fixed pieces, and climbers tend to over-trust this unknown gear, which might be damaged or inadequately placed. Relying on a single piece always carries significant risk. If you find yourself needing to retreat, use gear that you place yourself—either as the primary piece or to back up fixed gear. (*Sources: Yosemite National Park Search and Rescue and the Editors.*)

STRANDED | Weather
Inyo National Forest, White Mountains

On November 23, Hari Mix, a very experienced mountaineer (age 34), began a planned three-day traverse of the White Mountains, from White Mountain Peak to Boundary Peak. An exceptionally strong and unexpected wind event struck during the first night of the traverse, forcing the climber to descend extremely rough and loose terrain to the west to escape. Eventually, he called for help, though he ended up largely self-rescuing. The climber's instructive report is too in-depth to include here but can be found at *publications.americanalpineclub.org*. Mix also was interviewed for episode 51 of the Sharp End podcast: "Blown Away in California's White Mountains."

ROCKFALL FATALITIES
Sierra Nevada, Red Slate Mountain

On October 26, experienced climbers Jennifer Shedden (34) and Michelle Xue (22) approached Red Slate Mountain (13,156 feet), planning to climb its North Couloir. The route is a moderate snow couloir, approximately 1,500 feet high, that usually requires some ice and mixed climbing in autumn conditions. When the two did not check

The North Couloir of Red Slate Mountain in snowy October conditions. *Robert Yang*

in by late on October 27, the day they had planned to climb, friends alerted Mono County Search and Rescue, which deployed along with a California Highway Patrol helicopter. Search and rescue located the climbers on October 28, at about 12,400 feet, partway up the couloir, and determined both were deceased due to a large rockfall event.

ANALYSIS

Rockfall is common in Sierra couloirs, especially later in the day when temperatures rise. According to reports, the climbers planned to start their ascent before dawn to avoid this hazard. Members of Mono SAR observed no equipment failure, and the two climbers were found at a well-built and functioning anchor, where they apparently had been resting before continuing the climb. [*Editor's Note: There likely was no option in this case, but whenever possible, climbers should seek sheltered belay stances in couloirs, which are natural funnels for falling debris.*] (*Sources: Mono County Sheriff's Office and Rock and Ice.*)

STRANDED | Off-Route, Inadequate Gear, Injured Rescuer

Sierra Nevada, Mt. Emerson, Southeast Face

In the late afternoon of September 15, hikers on the Piute Pass Trail reported that they heard calls for help and saw people waving their arms on the rugged southeast face of Mt. Emerson (13,204 feet). Two Inyo County Search and Rescue members were dispatched to the scene, where they encountered one member of a three-person climbing party at the base of the face. He informed them that he and his two companions had been attempting the southeast face (III 5.4), but became lost and determined they could not continue. This climber was able to downclimb to the base to seek help, while his two companions were stranded several hundred feet up. During the night, the SAR team ascended about 1,000 feet up the face but were unable to locate the two stranded climbers. They decided to bivouac at 2:30 a.m.

At daybreak on the morning of September 16, the two rescuers continued searching for the stranded climbers, but eventually decided to retreat due to high winds and falling temperatures. During their retreat, at about 9:30 a.m., rocks fell from above (likely dislodged by the high wind), striking one rescuer on his right forearm and fracturing his radius and ulna, and on his right hip, causing deep soft-tissue damage. The team alerted the SAR base about their situation, and an additional team of eight SAR members was dispatched to assist the injured rescuer. Helicopter support was unavailable due to extremely high winds.

While the injured rescuer and his partner waited for help, they encountered the two purportedly stranded climbers coming up the southeast face, having elected to continue after bivouacking off-route. The two climbers were advised to wait with the injured SAR member and his teammate. Once the additional SAR members arrived on scene, they stabilized their injured teammate and lowered him approximately 1,000 feet to the bottom of the face. The climbers were also assisted to the bottom, using a combination of belayed downclimbing, lowering, and tandem rappelling.

ANALYSIS
The stranded climbers drastically underestimated their objective. Although the southeast face of Mt. Emerson has a modest rating of 5.4, the route-finding is not obvious and the route is long. The climbers left a rope and anchoring material at the base of the route, thinking they would not need it after the crux first pitch. Had they brought this gear with them, it might have given them the means to retreat. They also were unprepared for spending a long time on the route and became extremely cold as a result. The initial call for rescue was due to the combination of these factors.

The rockfall that injured the SAR member was a random, spontaneous event. Although the SAR hasty team recognized that conditions were deteriorating and decided to retreat, they fell victim to the objective dangers inherent to the mountains. Overall, this incident illustrates the importance of having the requisite experience for a given objective—and the skills and gear needed for self-rescue—and it is a reminder that rescuers expose themselves to risk of injury in order to assist stranded or injured parties. (*Source: Inyo County Search and Rescue.*)

RAPPEL ANCHOR FAILURE | Complacency, Fatigue
Sierra Nevada, Evolution Ridge Traverse

On July 1, I (43) was climbing with three partners near the midpoint of the Evolution Ridge Traverse (VI 5.9). It was our third day on this long, multi-peak traverse. During a scrambling section that afternoon, I caught up with my partners as they were discussing whether to downclimb or rappel a 10-foot steep section. They felt it would be an awkward downclimb with packs, and I did not investigate the descent myself. We decided to rope up and lower/rappel. There was just a single weathered-looking cordelette anchor in place, unlike the multiple slings at previous rappel anchors on the traverse. The likely reason for this is that most parties downclimb this section.

I slung a hay-bale-size rock with a new runner and belayed two of my partners down into the short gap before removing the runner. My other partner rappelled from just the weathered cordelette, but did not weight the rope fully. I then followed on rappel. After only a few feet, the cordelette snapped and I fell ten feet into the gap before tumbling another 40 to 50 feet.

I suffered fractures to my left clavicle, multiple neck vertebrae, and left metatarsal, along with a dislocated toe on my left foot, badly bruised and cut left heel/foot, cut upper left shin, and badly bruised left elbow. I was wearing a helmet, and this, along with my backpack, prevented more serious injury. We immediately contacted Inyo SAR, but due to high winds, they were unable to respond until the next morning, when I was hoisted and transported by helicopter to the hospital in Bishop.

ANALYSIS
This accident was caused by the failure of a single piece of cord that was not tested or backed up. I've never relied on gear in questionable/unknown condition before. It's possible my decision-making was compromised by the previous days of climbing.

My takeaways from the accident:

(1) Whenever possible, perform a standardized self-check and partner check of your system prior to climbing, rappelling, or during any transition.

(2) Consider resting or aborting the trip if feeling physically or mentally fatigued.

(3) Acclimatize sufficiently before strenuous and technical trips at high altitude.

(4) Back up and test single-piece fixed anchors. Avoid using weathered anchors if not backed up or replaced with new material.

(5) Avoid very short rappels if it would be reasonable to downclimb. (*Sources: Sean Reedy and the Editors.*)

FATAL FALL CAUSED BY ROCKFALL | Off-Route
High Sierra, Mt. Sill

On August 23, a party of four was attempting Mt. Sill in the Palisade Range via an unknown route (possibly the North Couloir). The climbers got off-route on the upper section and descended a short distance to reassess. At this point, a large block dislodged and fell, striking a 54-year-old male climber in the head and causing a tumbling fall of about 1,000 feet onto the upper Palisade Glacier. The remaining members downclimbed onto the glacier, confirmed their partner was deceased, and called for help via satellite messenger. They spent the night nearby, and the deceased climber was extracted from the glacier the next day by helicopter.

ANALYSIS
Loose rock is common throughout the Sierra Nevada but especially in the Palisade Range. Natural rockfall is common during the day as temperatures rise, as well as during high-wind events. Sometimes rockfall can be heard before it reaches climbers, but in other instances it occurs without warning.

All party members should familiarize themselves with their intended objective by studying topo maps, guidebooks, images, and other resources, because straying off-route increases the chances of encountering loose rock. In this case, the rockfall appears to have been natural. We have no information to suggest that the climbers could have predicted or avoided this event, highlighting the objective risks of technical travel in the Palisade Range. (*Source: Inyo County Search and Rescue.*)

SLIP ON ICE WHILE DESCENDING | Unable to Self-Arrest
High Sierra, Mt. Sill, North Couloir

Two 23-year-old males were descending the L-shaped snowfield below Mt. Sill's North Couloir in the late afternoon of October 20. Both were wearing helmets and crampons and using ice axes to descend extremely firm, sun-cupped, late-season snow. One climber slipped and tumbled approximately 400 feet, destroying his helmet and sustaining unknown but severe injuries. His partner notified the Inyo County Sheriff's Office via his Garmin inReach. A helicopter attempted to rescue the patient that night but was unable to land or hoist due to the high elevation (about 13,200 feet) and gusty north winds. The patient succumbed before rescuers could reach him.

On October 21, Inyo County Search and Rescue team members were inserted by helicopter near the patient's location. The helicopter hoisted the deceased climber, and the SAR team assisted his partner to a point where they could be extracted.

ANALYSIS
Late-season snow is typically very icy and can be difficult to ascend or descend safely, even for experienced climbers. A single misstep in firm conditions can easily lead to a sliding or tumbling fall that is nearly impossible to arrest. Climbers should consider running belays or snow-free routes if they have concerns about either their level of experience or the level of risk. (*Source: Inyo County Search and Rescue.*)

LOOSE ROCK
High Sierra, Mt. Whitney, Mountaineer's Route

Late on August 24, a 27-year-old female was descending the Mountaineer's Route on Mt. Whitney after summiting the peak. At about 13,900 feet, near the top of the big gully that characterizes much of this route, the climber dislodged a three-foot-diameter boulder that rolled over her entire body, fracturing her left tibia and fibula in addition to causing numerous soft-tissue injuries. Due to the time of day, high altitude, and confined terrain, a helicopter was unable to respond, and the patient and her party spent the night at the site of the accident. Her partners were able to shuttle supplies from their camp at Iceberg Lake, thus keeping her relatively warm and stable through the night.

The next morning, an Army National Guard Chinook helicopter transported seven Inyo County Search and Rescue (SAR) team members to the scene. One member was inserted via hoist near the patient's location to assess and stabilize her injuries. The remaining six SAR members were inserted 1,000 feet below the patient and climbed up to her. The patient was packaged into a litter, and the SAR team executed a single, rope, low-angle lower of about 250 feet to a location where a helicopter hoist was possible.

ANALYSIS
Loose rock is common throughout the Sierra Nevada, particularly after heavy winters like that of 2018–2019. Inyo SAR received numerous reports during the summer about substantial loose rock in the Mountaineer's Gully, a heavily traveled, narrow route constrained by steep walls that make it difficult to avoid falling or rolling rocks.

Calls for rescue that occur late in the day, at high elevations, in bad weather, or in confined terrain create serious safety concerns for helicopters and SAR teams, and the arrival of help may be significantly delayed. Parties should be prepared to shelter in place for up to 24 hours after initiating a call for rescue. Choosing reliable partners will help. Thanks to her partners' excellent care and ample overnight gear, the patient survived a night out at 13,900 feet with serious injuries. (*Source: Inyo County SAR.*)

FALL ON ROCK | Inadequate Protection, No Helmet
Southern California, Tahquitz, West Face

On July 28, a male climber (25) was leading the route Fingertrip (5.7) and fell when he was about 45 feet up the first pitch. Nearby climbers, many with medical and rescue training, heard the fall and quickly arrived on scene. They noted that three pieces had pulled out, including two nuts and a number 2 Camalot. A large nut had caught the climber's fall. None of the pieces that pulled had been extended, and a fixed piton on the route was not clipped.

The climber inverted during the fall and impacted a rock just above the ground. He sustained an open lower leg fracture and injuries to his face, and he lost consciousness, which he regained after being lowered to the ground. He was not wearing a helmet. (*Sources: Greg Davis and online report from another climber on the scene.*)

ANALYSIS

This route trends to the left along a downward-facing crack. In such scenarios, cams often are more forgiving of less-than-perfect placements than nuts are. Regardless, always keep in mind the direction of pull while placing protection. Extending each piece with a quickdraw or sling can stop the rope from shifting a piece out of its optimal placement. The fixed piton that was not clipped was old but still might have held a fall. A helmet might have minimized the climber's head injuries. (*Source: The Editors.*)

LEAD FALL ON ROCK | Pinned in Offwidth
Central Coast, Santa Barbara, Invisible Wall

On February 23, I (male, 31) went climbing with a small group of friends at the Invisible Wall in Santa Barbara. We are new climbers (less than two years), but I had taken several classes and regularly practiced rope skills at home. Midway through the afternoon, I tied in to lead Twice Stung and Forever Shy (5.10-), a 60-foot climb several grades below what I'd previously sent. The route sits about five feet to the left of a dihedral with an offwidth running up it. We hoped to top-rope the offwidth once I built an anchor at the top.

Above the halfway point, I hesitated for several minutes as I tried to figure out where to go. Seeing easier climbing above, I decided to just go for it. I fell and dropped about 15 feet, swung to the right, and ended up upside down, unconscious, and with my shoulder stuck in the offwidth. Despite wearing a helmet, I had a head wound that produced a significant amount of blood, and I was unable to be lowered. A nearby climber was able to free solo up an easier route to reach me, pull me out of the offwidth, and help lower me safely. I regained consciousness as I was righted. We were lucky to have a cell signal, and I was evacuated by helicopter to the hospital, where I was treated for a concussion, scalp laceration, blood loss, and a sprained thumb.

ANALYSIS

This incident was the result of my inexperience. While there were a number of components that caused injury (flipping upside down, swinging due to poor position, hitting the wall at just the right angle to cause a wound underneath my helmet, getting stuck while unconscious, etc.), many of these factors would have been mitigated or rendered moot with better awareness and technique that come with more experience. When confronted with more difficult climbing than anticipated, sometimes the prudent choice is to downclimb to a rest or back off entirely, rather than "just go for it" and risk injury. (*Sources: Tyler Johnson and the Editors.*)

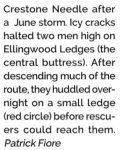

Crestone Needle after a June storm. Icy cracks halted two men high on Ellingwood Ledges (the central buttress). After descending much of the route, they huddled overnight on a small ledge (red circle) before rescuers could reach them. *Patrick Fiore*

COLORADO

STRANDED | Storm, Darkness, Inexperience
Sangre de Cristo Range, Crestone Needle, Ellingwood Ledges

On Friday, June 21, two climbers from Kansas (ages 23 and 30) drove up to the east side of the Sangre de Cristo Range. Their goal was the Ellingwood Ledges (a.k.a. Ellingwood Arête) on the east side of Crestone Needle. The 2,000-foot route ends at the summit of the 14,197-foot peak.

The next morning, under sunny skies, they started climbing at 9 a.m. via the route's direct start. Their iPhone weather app showed a forecast of "partly cloudy with a 20% chance of showers." Enjoying warm weather and dry rock, the duo made good time cruising the easy 5th class pitches at the bottom and the grassy and rocky 3rd- and 4th-class ledges in the middle of the route. However, at the route's crux, just a few hundred feet below the summit, the 5.7 to 5.9 cracks (depending on exact route) were filled with ice. Clad in rock shoes and with no ice axes, they couldn't climb past the thin ribbons of ice. Meanwhile, the sky turned gray as, unbeknownst to the pair, a strong winter-like storm was barreling in from the west.

Around 4 p.m. the storm hit, with intense snow showers along with thunder and lightning. The pair put on their light fleece jackets and waterproof jackets. With visibility dropping to 30 feet, they kept trying to climb, thinking safety would be gained by going over the top and descending the standard route. (The 3rd-class normal route up and down Crestone Needle is exposed and tricky to follow, and has stranded climbers even in the best weather.) Eventually, realizing they could not go up, the pair called the Custer County Sheriff's Office to request assistance. It was about 5:30 p.m.

Custer County Search and Rescue (CCSAR) began planning for a possible technical rescue. The climbers started down, building rappel anchors and occasionally downclimbing, a descent they described as "terrifying." They made steady progress and continued to give updates to CCSAR. (Cell service is very good high on the Crestones.) At approximately 9:30 p.m. and at 13,030 feet, soaked and shivering hard, and nearly out of gear to build anchors, the pair grew concerned their fatigue could affect their safety if they continued. In a call with CCSAR, a senior member told them not to continue down if they were not completely confident in their anchors. They decided to stop and wait for morning on a snow-covered ledge about as wide as a lawn chair.

Given the complexity of the situation, CCSAR began planning a parallel rescue effort: one ground-based and another by helicopter hoist. Members of various other rescue teams started toward the area to help, and a line of communication was opened with the Colorado Army National Guard (COANG).

High on the mountain, light snow continued to fall until about 1 a.m., and then, as the skies cleared, the temperature dropped into the lower 20s (F). Their sodden clothing froze hard and their joints turned stiff. They had found no gear placements, so they had no anchor. Afraid to even stand up for fear they might fall, they stayed put. The two were so miserable and scared that they each called parents and siblings to say good-bye, thinking they might die before sunrise.

By 3 a.m., rescue teams started to arrive at CCSAR's base in Westcliffe. An hour later, over 20 mountain rescuers from four counties were hiking toward the base of Ellingwood Arête. All the while, CCSAR liaised with the National Guard to coordinate a helicopter extraction utilizing two Alpine Rescue Team hoist rescue technicians. Weather conditions were questionable, and it was not until well after sunrise that the helicopter mission became a "go." After a 130-mile flight, Black Hawk 529 out of Buckley Air Force Base arrived overhead at about 9:45 a.m. and determined a hoist insert and extraction was possible.

MAKING THE CALL: CELL PHONES AND RESCUES

In the Crestone Needle rescue, the ability to maintain two-way communications with rescuers was critical. The stranded climbers not only could call for help, they also were able to discuss their situation with rescuers, and the conversations with rescuers and family helped keep them motivated during a long, cold night.

To preserve battery power, rescuers instructed the pair to limit outside calls. Too often, people who call for help start calling other people as well, draining their battery and leaving rescuers with no way to stay in touch. (It should go without saying that batteries shouldn't be wasted on Instagram or checking email.) This pair limited their calls and preserved one phone throughout the night.

It's not just battery life that's at stake in deciding who to call in such a situation, because an accident in the mountains affects many people. Unsure they would survive the night, the two climbers called their families to say "good-byes," an experience that caused huge swings in emotions. At one point, a family member's call went to voicemail, and only hours later did one of the climbers answer another call and report that both were still alive. To unexpectedly be talking over a phone to a loved one who is sure they are on the verge of death generates a level of fear and sadness that is difficult to describe. Fortunately, these climbers and their families got a second chance.

– Dale Atkins

Two rescue techs were lowered to the stranded climbers. Other than being very cold, stiff, hungry, and thirsty, the climbers were in remarkably good condition. The morning sun had thawed and dried their clothes, and warmed their spirits. The two were helped into rescue harnesses, and when the Black Hawk returned, the climbers and rescuers were hoisted two at a time and flown to CCSAR's base in Westcliffe. By 2:45 p.m., all the ground teams had returned safely to Westcliffe, ending a 22-hour mission.

ANALYSIS

The two climbers were capable multi-pitch crag climbers who aspired to do their first alpine or big-mountain route. They had the skill to climb this route in summer conditions; however, the preceding winter had been one of Colorado's snowiest in many years. Though the calendar said late June, snow and ice on the high mountains was similar to mid-May. The arrival of the storm only worsened the situation.

The storm had been well forecasted for the mountains, but the pair did not get the right forecast. Many phone apps present weather for nearby towns, so the climbers got the forecast for Westcliffe, located in the valley to the northeast of the mountain. Then they typed in "Crestone" and another benign forecast popped up—however, this forecast was for the hamlet of Crestone, low in a valley on the west side of the peak. Seeing two good forecasts, the climbers were confident. But there was a very different forecast for the peaks 6,000 feet higher. [Editor's Note: 14ers.com links to NOAA spot forecasts for each of the Colorado 14ers.]

The climbers had a good alpine rack but left nearly all of it as they rappelled and downclimbed nearly 1,000 feet of snow-covered rock and grass. In their packs they carried shell jackets, beanies, gloves, and good socks—barely enough protection. They climbed in rock shoes and carried light trail shoes for the descent. In a typical summer, these shoes would have been fine, but had they reached the summit, their descent off a very snowy and icy Broken Hand Pass would have been difficult.

To their credit, these climbers kept their wits and survived a miserable night in a very exposed spot. They tried very hard to self-rescue and did a phenomenal job to descend as far as they did.

The role of luck—good and bad—plays a much larger role than we often acknowledge in such situations. In the Sangre de Cristo Range, the weather cleared soon after midnight, leaving the climbers with drying conditions. Further north in Colorado's central and northern mountains, the storm continued all night, and upwards of two feet of snow fell. These two put themselves in a place to be lucky when they wisely decided to stop. Surviving a miserable night is always easier than surviving a fall. (Sources: Dale Atkins, Alpine Rescue Team and Colorado Hoist Rescue Team, and Jonathan Wiley and Patrick Fiore of Custer County SAR.)

FALL ON ROCK | Protection Pulled Out, Loose Rock
Durango Area, Cascade Canyon

I was climbing with three friends in Cascade Canyon on Fourth of July weekend. Luke and Ben had climbed in the area before, but Will and I (female, 20) had not. Will and I chose a route called Funky Crack (5.8 trad) that was well within both of our abilities. Will led the route first and left the protection that he had placed. I climbed it after him, re-placing all the gear to work on my own placements. I remember clipping one last nut before starting to traverse over to the upper anchors, at the top of the cliff. The limestone was loose and crumbly. The last thing that I remember was calling down to Will and asking, "Hey! Where did you go from here?" I am guessing my hand slipped on the loose rock, and I fell. I was told the rock where my last nut was placed basically exploded from the force of my fall. With the nut gone, there was too much slack in the system to stop me from hitting the ground 60 feet below. I was told that I also clipped a ledge with my feet as I fell.

Somehow I landed on my feet but had so much momentum that I catapulted forward and hit my jaw on the rocky ground. Will and Ben, who are both wilderness emergency medical technicians (WEMTs), went to work stabilizing me while Luke ran to the top of the canyon to call search and rescue. Both of my lungs collapsed before SAR could get to me, but Will performed a needle decompression and was able to keep me conscious. I was taken in an ambulance to the Purgatory ski resort, then helicoptered from there to a hospital in Grand Junction, where preliminary scans determined that I needed to be in a Level I trauma center. From Grand Junction, I was flown to a hospital in Denver.

I fractured my left medial malleolus and calcaneus, shattered my right calcaneus, fractured my right tibia and femur, fractured my pelvis in five places, sustained an L2 compression fracture, fractured four ribs, fractured my jaw in multiple places, lost four teeth and fractured seven more, and sustained a labyrinthine concussion.

ANALYSIS

I had never climbed in the area and was not familiar with the quality of the limestone. Had I known it was poor on this route, I would not have chosen to climb it. I was a new trad leader, but I don't think that was a big factor in my fall. If I had tested the rock more, I might have noticed that my last placement wasn't in super-solid rock, but that didn't cross my mind at the time. [*Editor's Note: This climb is considered reasonably protected until a midway anchor, but has sparse protection in the upper section, where the climber fell.*] (Source: Ella Hall.)

LEDGE FALL | Inadequate Protection
Black Canyon of the Gunnison National Park, North Chasm View Wall

Around midday on October 5, a male climber fell approximately 25 feet while leading Stoned Oven, a multi-pitch 5.11+ climb on North Chasm View Wall. The climber fell on easier terrain after completing an airy traverse on the sixth pitch of the ascent, and he hit a right-facing ramp, sustaining a leg injury that was later determined to be a displaced distal tibia-fibula fracture.

Around 1:30 p.m., park visitors reported they had heard yelling for help from inside the canyon. The climbing ranger, Tom Schaefer, directed a ranger on the opposite rim of the canyon to use binoculars and a spotting scope to locate the injured climber and his partner. They determined that the climbing party was self-rescuing to the bottom of the canyon by rappelling the route, with the injured climber using only one leg. Schaefer attempted to contact the party from the rim with a megaphone but was unable to establish communication. He activated the volunteer SAR team and began to prepare a rigging plan to assist the climber out of the canyon if necessary.

Schaefer and two volunteer SAR nurses met the climbing party as they reached the bottom of the canyon around 6 p.m. The injured climber was unable to walk, making it impossible to hike out via the Cruise Gully. At this point, a decision was made to conduct a rope raise of the injured climber the next day. The two SAR nurses stayed overnight with the climber, providing gear, medical care, and pain management. The next day, 25 volunteers from Black Canyon SAR, Ouray SAR, Rigging for Rescue, and Crested Butte Mountain Rescue assisted with the rope raise.

The Black Canyon is about 1,800 feet deep in the area of North Chasm View Wall. Once the haul system was organized, it took two hours to raise the injured climber and a rescuer from the bottom. *NPS Photo*

At 7 a.m., a Dual Capability Twin Tension Rope System was set up on the rim, using two 360-meter ropes followed by two 180-meter ropes. While the injured climber and SAR team sheltered under an overhanging cave feature, some loose rock was cleaned off the lower portion of the route. The litter was then lowered to the bottom and the injured climber hauled to the rim. The entire operation took six hours, with the raise itself taking two hours.

ANALYSIS

The climber fell a long way on easier terrain, and he later acknowledged he should have placed another piece to minimize the potential fall. Due to the technical terrain and remoteness of the Black Canyon's rim, response times can be elongated. There is no cell phone reception, and even personal locator beacons may not function properly inside the narrow canyon. The only ways rangers can track who is in the canyon is the self-registration wilderness-use permit system. A large majority of rescues in the canyon are reported in late afternoon, and most inner canyon rescues require overnight patient care while a rescue plan is organized and conducted the next day. The lesson is that a conservative approach is required while climbing in this environment. (*Sources: Tom Schaefer, climbing ranger, and the injured climber.*)

FALL ON ROCK | Broken Hold, Protection Pulled Out
Rocky Mountain National Park, Hallett Peak

My husband, Travis, and I were climbing the Culp-Bossier Route (8 pitches, 5.8+) on Hallett Peak on July 7. Five friends of ours were climbing adjacent routes. I'd done Pervertical Sanctuary (5.11a) on the Diamond of Longs Peak two days prior, and Culp-Bossier was supposed to be an easy day.

On the sixth pitch, I got distressed because I thought I was off-route. [*Editor's Note: This pitch, rated 5.6, is notoriously difficult to follow and sparsely protected if you stray off-route.*] I was scared because this was a fairly serious pitch, with large runouts and bad gear. I thought I saw a way out above me: a big hold and an easy-looking traverse to what I thought was the route. I got about 15 feet above my last piece (a fixed piton), grabbed the jug, and the hold broke. I fell backward to the piton, which then ripped out. The nut below that ripped as well. The next piece (a number 0.5 Camalot) was quite far below that, but it eventually caught me. I had fallen about 70 feet headfirst. My helmet was destroyed, but I was alive.

I came to a stop not far from my husband; he lowered me and I swung across the ledge to him. We both cried together, and I told him I loved him maybe 100 times. He and I made a plan for self-rescue and began to execute it. Soon, however, two of our friends rappelled down to us and began helping us to the base of the cliff, which we reached after about two hours of rappels. I hiked out (approximately 2.5 miles) with medic support. I had a concussion, a broken wrist, and a deep elbow laceration.

ANALYSIS
I got really lucky, and I'm so thankful to have amazing friends who facilitated a safe and fast self-rescue from the cliff. Some lessons learned include:

Know your route well. Route-finding on Hallett is known to be challenging. I have climbed hundreds of routes, but I don't think I've ever been as lost as I was on Culp-Bossier. I should have made more of an effort to figure out this particular pitch before setting out.

Pay attention to rappel stations while you climb. One of my friends who came to our rescue had climbed the route twice previously and knew where the rappel stations were. This saved us time and gear on the descent.

Don't trust fixed pitons. I had so little gear on the pitch that I was ecstatic when I found a piton. It gave me unwarranted peace of mind, and without it I may have taken more care in testing the holds. However, it is possible the piton slowed my fall before it failed.

Know self-rescue techniques and wilderness first aid. I have taken multiple self-rescue classes and first-aid courses. My husband is certified in wilderness first aid, and we have reviewed self-rescue together. This enabled us to quickly come up with a plan and calm each other down. Thankfully, we had friends nearby who came to our aid, as it would have been quite time-consuming to retreat with one rope, and we would have lost a lot of gear. (*Source: Margie Root.*)

THE SHARP END (EPISODE 46): *Margie Root and Leslie Gains-Germain, one of the friends who assisted in the Hallett Peak rescue, were interviewed about this incident for "Pitching In: Group Rescue on Hallett Peak" on the Sharp End podcast.*

FATAL FALL ON ROCK | Off-Route, Unable to Clip Bolt
Poudre Canyon, Eden Area

Mitch, Hunter, and I arrived at the Eden Area, a roadside crag, at around 2 p.m. on May 18. Mitch elected to lead Tree of Knowledge (5.10b sport), and I put up the route East of Eden (5.9 trad). We swapped top-rope belays and discussed our dinner plans as the sun began to drop behind the hills. As we were packing up, I saw Mitch racking up draws and eyeing the route Fish and Whistle (5.11a/b sport), which climbs the arête above the road. I had done this route during my spring break trip, and we discussed the low crux and the potential for ground fall, but Mitch decided he wanted to give it a try.

This route starts only a few feet off the highway, so I built a ground anchor for myself to prevent us from rolling into the road in the event of an early fall. We did our final checks, and Mitch started up the route. He clipped the first two bolts without issue and started through the crux. He took a short (one meter) fall at the crux and rested for a moment. He then proceeded to make quick work of the crux and continued toward the third bolt. Here, he struggled to find a good stance to clip and quickly went from looking strong and calm to distressed. He continued up and right until the waist of his harness was level with the third bolt. He managed to attach a quickdraw to the hanger and tried to clip the rope. He nearly had the rope clipped when he fell off.

I felt the rope go tight and was pulled off the ground. Because of his position, he fell slightly back and impacted a rock outcropping, with the back of his head and the upper part of his torso striking first. He was unconscious, not breathing, had no detectable heartbeat, was bleeding profusely from his head, and I strongly suspected he had spinal or neck injuries.

Fish and Whistle in Poudre Canyon, with the second and third bolt locations shown. The belay was on the bushy pedestal. *Victor Pinto*

I took command of the situation and instructed Hunter to stabilize Mitch's head and neck, and I lowered the two of them from the raised area where I was belaying to flatter ground near the highway. I had a good base of first-aid skills, and I performed CPR on Mitch for approximately 15 to 20 minutes, which resulted in a detectable heartbeat and him breathing under his own power. I quickly assessed Mitch for any other treatable injuries, but found nothing. The bleeding from his head had slowed significantly, and he appeared to be breathing on his own. Blood had been pooling in his airway, so we monitored him extremely closely to keep him from choking.

We did not have cell reception, but were able to flag down several passing cars within minutes. Eventually an ambulance and several vehicles from the Larimer County Sheriff's Office arrived on scene. A helicopter later landed on the road and brought additional personnel and equipment. Unfortunately, Mitch slowly began to deteriorate; his breathing slowed, pulse faded, and he became completely unresponsive. Hunter and I were ushered away, and we were sitting behind our car, away from the scene, when one of the paramedics came over and informed us Mitch had passed.

ANALYSIS

Mitch (age 22) and I were regular climbing and training partners. He was strong, often flashing my gym projects and placing in local climbing competitions. But most of his climbing had been done in the gym, and though his basic skills were pretty solid, he had much to learn about outdoor climbing. Fish and Whistle would have been his hardest sport climb to date. Learning to read the rock, where the best line and clipping stances are found, and how to back off when things turn ugly are vital skills that I don't think Mitch had fully developed. It's also possible that a long stick clip could have been used to clip the first few bolts, in order to minimize ground fall potential.

Most climbers doing this route make crux moves onto the left side of the arête and then reach a good hold for clipping the third bolt; Mitch stayed in a corner on the right until the third bolt was at his waist but out of reach. After this tragic accident, the local climber who bolted this route decided to add an optional bolt on the right to protect climbers who stray onto this path. (*Sources: Eric Burrell and the Editors.*)

FATAL FALL FROM CLIFF TOP | Loose Rock
Boulder Canyon, Bell Buttress

In midmorning on August 24, a 50-year-old male climber fell approximately 120 feet from the top of Bell Buttress, causing fatal injuries. The man and his climbing partner had just completed the second pitch of Cosmosis (5.10a) and were searching for a bolted rappel station. The pair unroped and began scrambling climber's left toward the anchor. The climber stated to his partner that the terrain looked easy and that he felt comfortable traversing it, but as they were scrambling he fell. His partner didn't witness the fall, but other climbers in the area described a rock dislodging under the climber as he was scrambling.

Climbers at the crag reached the patient on a ledge and found him unresponsive. A Boulder ranger responded, and the climber was pronounced dead at the scene.

ANALYSIS
Most parties do only the classic first pitch of Cosmosis, which can be descended via a single lower or rappel from a bolted anchor. Since the second pitch doesn't have a fixed anchor at its top, continuing up that pitch meant choosing among several descent options, including the scramble to reach a rappel station to the east or a walk-off to the southwest. Nearly every year, this publication records one or more fatal unroped falls from the tops of cliffs, often as climbers search for descent routes. It's not uncommon to encounter loose rock or slippery vegetation and dirt on cliff-top edges. If a secure path cannot be identified and followed, consider staying on belay until the anchor or descent trail is reached. (*Sources: Boulder County Sheriff's Office, online post from the climber's partner, and the Editors.*)

GROUND FALL | Protection Unclipped from Rope
Boulder Canyon, Animal World

On July 7, at approximately 2 p.m., my fiancé John Luebbers (34) and I (32) were attempting a tight dihedral called We Don't Do Crack, a single-pitch 5.8 with a tricky start. I had placed one piece (number 0.5 C4 Camalot) about six to eight feet off the ground, with an unextended alpine draw (the route went straight up so rope drag was not an issue). There was a slick hand jam that I couldn't stick, despite having done it about an hour before, and I fell about two feet. The gear caught my fall as expected. The piece did not move and was still in a textbook placement on solid rock. I tried the move again with the same result. I checked the security of the piece after the second fall; everything looked fine. On the third try I fell again and, in a freak occurrence, the rope-end carabiner on my alpine draw opened and the rope disconnected from the draw.

I fell about eight feet and hit the deck, then tumbled over a series of boulders down the climbers' trail another 25 feet, stopping just shy of a bushy cliff. Some willows were the only thing stopping me from tumbling far down to the road below.

John had braced for my fall, but when the rope unweighted after the cam was unclipped, he lost his balance. As I fell, I pulled him down the trail with me. He tumbled over a four-foot boulder and stopped. When I sat up, the rope-end carabiner was attached to my rope while my cam and the rest of the alpine draw still sat in the crack.

Two nearby climbers with medical training helped me tape my leg and clean our wounds before assisting us down the trail to our vehicle. Both John and I had abrasions and bruises, and I also sustained whiplash, but X-rays did not show further injuries.

ANALYSIS

Initially I suspected I might have grabbed the carabiner in panic as I fell and that might have caused the gate to open. However, after re-creating the scenario on an indoor wall, this does not seem likely. The most likely scenario is the carabiner spun so that, before or during my fall, my tie-in knot, my body, the sling, or the rope caused the gate to open, similar to falling on a backclipped quickdraw, and resulted in the carabiner disconnecting from the sling. This would be a rare occurrence, but within the realm of possibility.

Grivel Twin Gate carabiner.

Since the accident, we've been using special carabiners with two opposing gates for our first piece or any piece near a crux move. [*Editor's Note: A locking carabiner is also a good option.*] While my ground fall might have been unavoidable, my 25-foot tumble after hitting the deck could have been shortened if we had anchored the belayer so he wouldn't be pulled off balance. Even in seemingly inconsequential terrain, the momentum of such falls should not be underestimated.

Both John and I were wearing helmets, and we suspect we might have been more seriously injured as we tumbled over the rocks if we hadn't been. (*Source: Meg Atteberry.*)

THE SHARP END (EPISODE 50): *Meg and John share their story and the aftermath of these events in "Trouble in the Belaytionship" on the Sharp End podcast.*

FALL ON ROCK | Loose Rock, Inadequate Protection
Eldorado Canyon, Redgarden Wall

On May 17, at approximately 7 p.m., two experienced climbers set out to climb Swanson Arête, a long 5.5, after doing several difficult single-pitch routes on Redgarden Wall. The plan was to simul-climb the route and descend the East Slabs of Redgarden to return to their car. To reach Swanson Arête, which begins from Red Ledge partway up the cliff, Climber 1 started with the first pitch of the Great Zot (5.8+). Above this, he clipped a bolted anchor at the top of neighboring West Chimney route and traversed the broad Red Ledge to the base of Swanson Arête. While navigating these ledges or the start of Swanson Arête, the climber pulled off a microwave-size block and fell, eventually coming to a stop on Red Ledge. He had placed no gear after the bolted anchor.

Although unresponsive at first, Climber 1 was vocal after 15 seconds and quickly self-diagnosed a broken leg. Still on the ground, Climber 2 called 911 immediately. Given the uncertainty about a spinal injury, Climber 2 opted to wait for rescuers instead of trying to lower Climber 1 to the ground.

Another party was descending West Chimney, and one of the climbers untied, soloed the last third of the West Chimney (5.6) to reach the injured climber, and then fixed a rope that could be used by rescuers to reach Climber 1. Rocky Mountain Rescue Group responded, reaching the site within an hour of the initial 911 call. Climber 1 sustained a broken femur, spinal fracture, broken wrist, four broken ribs, and a punctured lung; he has made a full recovery and returned to climbing.

ANALYSIS

This accident is difficult to analyze, since the belayer could not see the climber fall (he just heard "falling"), and Climber 1 does not remember details. Our crags are dynamic places, constantly shifting. Even on well-traveled classics, we must remain vigilant in evaluating rock and potentially adjust our tactics in loose terrain by placing more protection or establishing intermediate belays. The choice to simul-climb or link pitches increases the risk of long falls and ledge falls. (*Source: Climber 2.*)

FALL ON ROCK | Inadequate Protection for Second
Eldorado Canyon, The Bastille

On September 9 at about 9 a.m., my friend Austin and I set out to climb Werk Supp on the north face of the Bastille. I led the first pitch (5.8+), placing protection only where I felt that I needed it. The pitch ends by pulling over a slight bulge, protected by a cam, onto a slanted ledge. There is a bolted anchor about 10 feet to the left on this ledge and at a downward angle. I traversed the ledge to belay from this anchor, so I was located slightly lower and far to the left of my last piece of protection.

At the final bulge, Austin removed my last cam and attempted the finishing mantel move for about 10 minutes, then fell off and took a significant pendulum swing onto a rock bulge directly below where I was belaying. We both heard a pop, and Austin yelled that his foot was in intense pain.

I rigged a 3-to-1 assisted haul to bring him up to the belay ledge, so I could inspect his ankle. It had immediately become very swollen, but at the time we only suspected a severe sprain. I lowered Austin directly to the ground and then rappelled to join him. Fortunately, the base of the route is only a short walk from the car. Austin initially chose to rest his ankle for a few days, but eventually decided to get an X-ray, which revealed a shattered right talus and a torn sheath of the peroneus longus and brevis tendons.

ANALYSIS

Austin had only climbed outside five times and never on anything this difficult. As I was climbing, I was more focused on protecting the route for me than for the

person who would be following. Placing another piece of protection after the final difficult move, before the downward traverse, would have protected the follower from a significant swing. Another option would be to build an anchor directly above the first pitch, rather than using the bolted anchor off to the side. [*Editor's Note: Many climbers exit this pitch to the left via a lower traverse, heading more directly to the bolted anchor; this is safer for the second climber.*] It's also worth noting that the climber initially only suspected a sprain, but the injury

Reconstruction of a 3-to-1 haul rigged on the Werk Supp anchor to help an injured climber to the ledge. The Grigri acts as a progress-capture device; a plaquette in guide mode serves the same purpose. *Bill Kinter*

actually involved a fracture that required surgery. Neglecting to seek medical attention for even longer could have led to further complications. (*Source: Bill Kinter.*)

ROCKFALL | Crowded Cliff
Eldorado Canyon, Redgarden Wall

My partner and I (age 23) decided to climb Rewritten (5.7) in Eldorado Canyon State Park on Saturday, December 7. We started later in the day, arriving at the park around 10 a.m., because the morning was cold. The park was relatively empty, but there were three other parties in the small area around Rewritten: one starting the first pitch of Rewritten, one preparing to climb West Chimney, and one beginning Swanson Arête, starting on the Red Ledge.

As I was flaking the rope at the base of the Rewritten, a climber on Swanson Arête yelled "rock!" and I saw a basketball-size rock coming down. I ran toward the base of the climb and got in the fetal position, thinking the rock was moving outward. The rock hit a ledge and exploded, and a tennis ball–size fragment hit my right elbow. I took my shell off to find my arm covered in blood. I stepped away from the wall about ten meters and pulled out a small med kit I had in my backpack. As my partner was cleaning the blood off my cut, a golf ball–size rock landed about six inches from my big toe (I didn't have my climbing shoes on yet). I panicked for about 30 seconds but was able to calm down and move further from the wall.

During this time, the party climbing Rewritten had continued up the route, with the leader almost at the first belay ledge. The belayer then noticed that some of their rope, still on the ground, had been severely damaged by the rockfall. Fortunately, that portion of the rope wasn't in the belay system yet. The climber decided to downclimb the route. We headed back to the car.

ANALYSIS

Rockfall is an objective hazard at most cliffs, but some areas are more prone than others. The area around Rewritten is characterized by large belay ledges covered in loose rock. Falling rocks are liable to bounce off ledges and can land anywhere, including many meters into the nearby woods. The climber on Swanson did yell "rock" very audibly, which gave us some warning.

Rewritten is one of the most popular routes in one of the most popular climbing areas in greater Denver. I made an assumption that the route wouldn't be as busy in December and after recent snow. It would have been better to arrive earlier or even decide on a different route after seeing how busy it was.

After a rockfall incident, it's a good idea to re-flake and inspect your rope. The climber on Rewritten had almost reached the top of the first pitch before the belayer noticed the damaged section of rope. (*Source: Anonymous injured climber.*)

FATAL GROUND FALL | Miscommunication, Lowering Error
Clear Creek Canyon, Other Critters Area

On June 6 at 12:56 p.m., the Alpine Rescue Team responded to the report of an 18-year-old female climber who had fallen at the Other Critters area. Initial reports indicated the climber had fallen a significant distance and was unresponsive. While Alpine was en route, Clear Creek County EMS personnel were able to access the fallen climber and confirm she had not survived the fall. It was estimated the climber had fallen a total of 160 feet.

After the evacuation of the fallen climber, two climbers from Alpine Rescue were able to access the route (Labby, 5.9 sport) and recover the climbing gear still on the wall. The members noted the climber's anchor setup was appropriate, all quickdraws were placed properly, and no equipment failure was observed.

In conjunction with the Clear Creek Country Sheriff's Office, Alpine Rescue was able to reconstruct the events leading up to the climber's fall.

Somewhere between 9 and 10 a.m., Climber 1 and Climber 2 arrived at the Other Critters area with the intent of climbing several routes. Their first route was a three-pitch bolted 5.6 called Yellow Dog Dingo. Prior to leaving the ground, the pair discussed a system to manage the belays. Climber 1 would lead each pitch, and after an anchor was properly established, the leader would tug on the rope two times as the indication to Climber 2 to take her off belay and prepare to climb. The pair agreed to this system based on the crag's proximity to busy Highway 6 and their fear that verbal communication would be difficult. Climbers 1 and 2 successfully climbed all three pitches of Yellow Dog Dingo with this system and then rappelled to the base of the route, where they had left their backpacks.

Climber 1 suggested they climb Labby next. The route starts on a wide ledge to climber's right and above the start of Yellow Dog Dingo. Climber 1 set up to lead the route. The plan for the route was identical to the system previously used: Two rope tugs meant Climber 1 was safe and Climber 2 should take her off belay and prepare to climb. Climber 1 believed Labby to be another multi-pitch route, and she left the ground with the intention of tying in to the anchor and belaying Climber 2 to the top. However, upon reaching the anchor, Climber 1 realized Labby was only a single-pitch route (about 80 feet high). Climber 1 attached her anchor slings to the bolts and clipped her end of the rope to the master point. It's unclear if any verbal communication to Climber 2 was attempted. Climber 1, thinking she was still on belay, sat back on the rope to be lowered and fell.

From Climber 2's belay position, she could not see Climber 1 at the anchor and was under the impression Climber 1 would belay her to the top. After Climber 1 disappeared from view, Climber 2 felt two tugs on the rope. Based on the system they had agreed to use, she took Climber 1 off belay. As Climber 2 was tying herself into the rope, she heard a scream and saw Climber 1 fall.

Based on the above reconstruction, it is likely that Climber 1 pulled up on the rope as she set up the anchor for lowering. Having no view of the anchor and not hearing any verbal communication, Climber 2 felt these rope pulls and interpreted them as Climber 1's signal to go off belay.

ANALYSIS

It's important to highlight several oversights by the climbers in this tragic accident. First, had the pair known Labby was a single-pitch route, they might have chosen a different rope management system. Records indicate the pair had consulted Mountain Project prior to climbing Labby but failed to identify it as a single-pitch climb. Second, a non-verbal system for belay management during multi-pitch climbing is useful, but relying solely on rope tugs can lead to problems. Movements in the rope such as clipping, climbing, and constructing an anchor can be misconstrued as off-belay signals. Combined, these mistakes led to the fatal accident. Such incidents reinforce the importance of double-checking the belay before lowering by testing the system with body weight before you unclip from the anchor, especially if you cannot hear or see the belayer below.

Accidents such as this have more than one victim that requires attention. The American Alpine Club offers resources to survivors through the Climbing Grief Fund. Additional information can be found at *americanalpineclub.org/grieffund*. (*Sources: Paul "Woody" Woodward, Gerrit Padgham, and Curt Honcharik, Alpine Rescue Team.*)

FALL FROM TYROLEAN TRAVERSE
Clear Creek Canyon, East Colfax

In early summer, during the annual runoff from mountain snowmelt, a climber crossed swollen Clear Creek on a semi-permanent Tyrolean traverse; he was returning to the roadside East Colfax area after climbing on the opposite side of the river. The traverse ropes were anchored about eight feet up in a tree, and a short home made ladder descended to the rocks below. As the climber was attempting to escape the traverse ropes, he fell into the river and was swept downstream. Other climbers ran down the bank to assist but were unable to reach him. Fortunately, after carrying the climber about 150 yards, the current pushed him into some rocks by the shore and he was rescued (unharmed but badly shaken) before entering bigger rapids.

ANALYSIS

Several crags in this canyon are accessed by established Tyrolean traverses. Climbers attach themselves to these ropes in various ways, but no matter which method is used, three principles will assure greater safety: 1) Your connection to the rope should be backed up and should not rely on a single quickdraw or sling; 2) Your pack should be attached separately, giving you greater maneuverability; and 3) You should remain clipped into the ropes or an anchor until you are on firm ground—a long sling or personal anchor system (PAS) is useful for this purpose. This particular traverse has an unusually difficult access/exit on its east side; a climber fell here in 2014 while struggling to attach a pulley to the ropes and shattered his femur. (*Sources: Eyewitness and the Editors.*)

LOWERING ERROR | Inexperience
Clear Creek Canyon, Sushi Slab

On July 27 at 2:18 p.m., the Alpine Rescue Team responded to the report of a fallen climber (male, early 20s) at Sushi Slab. The climber was discovered with a lower leg injury and unable to walk. Due to the location of the crag (several hundred feet up a steep gully filled with loose rock), the climber was loaded into a litter and a technical evacuation was completed down the gully to the roadway. At the hospital, a lower leg fracture was confirmed.

Prior to the fall, the climbers were attempting Dragon Roll (5.5 sport climb). The male climber had successfully led the pitch, set up a top-rope anchor, and was in the process of being lowered. As he was removing the quickdraw from the highest bolt before the anchor, his belay partner lost her footing, causing her to lose control of the brake strand. The climber fell approximately 40 feet. The belayer was using an ATC-style belay device.

ANALYSIS
The pair of climbers, a 20-year-old male and 13-year-old female, were brother and sister and had been climbing in the gym regularly. They had not climbed outside together prior to this incident. Though a climbing gym provides a reasonably safe environment to practice climbing skills, the natural environment presents risks that novice climbers may overlook (weather, route conditions) or underappreciate (importance of adequate belay stances). Additionally, assisted-braking devices, though not foolproof, can offer an extra margin of safety when belaying and lowering. (*Source: Curt Honcharik and Steve Wilson, Alpine Rescue Team.*)

FALL ON ROCK | Inadequate Protection, No Helmet
Clear Creek Canyon, Creekside

In the afternoon of November 9, the Alpine Rescue Team responded to the report of a 22-year-old male climber who had fallen at the Creekside climbing area. The climber was on the last pitch of Black Gold (5 pitches, 5.7+), approximately 300 feet off the ground, when the fall took place. He was not wearing a helmet and was unconscious for several minutes.

Nearby climbers were able to access and assist the injured climber to the ground, where first responders were staged. Clear Creek Fire Authority assisted in the evacuation by using a ladder truck to ferry the injured climber across the creek. At the hospital, the climber was diagnosed with a head injury, broken clavicle, two compression fractures of the spine, and various contusions, but was expected to make a full recovery.

ANALYSIS

After a few weeks had passed, members of Alpine Rescue Team were able to reach the subject and conduct an in-depth interview. After climbing pitch four, the two climbers reached a bolted belay stance under a small overhang. Unclear on the route ahead, one of the climbers agreed to traverse out right of the overhang to explore the options. Prior to leaving the belay, the lead climber pulled up approximately 30 feet of rope and tied in directly to the anchor. The belayer remained at the anchor station but was not belaying the other climber. The leader traversed right about 20 feet with no protection, and then, realizing the potential for a large fall, he attempted to place a cam, but he slipped during the placement and fell.

There are several takeaways from the accident. First, had the climbers surveyed their surroundings and studied route descriptions more closely, they may have realized the route goes almost directly

Rescuers deployed a ladder truck from U.S. Highway 6 to quickly ferry an injured climber across Clear Creek, avoiding a long, strenuous litter carry. *Tyler Zito | Alpine Rescue Team*

through the overhang above the belay and not out right, as they believed. Both Mountain Project (www.mountainproject.com) and the local climbing guidebook have ample descriptions and photos of this pitch. Additionally, several system errors were made as the lead climber traversed from the belay. The belayer should have remained in the system to prevent slack in the rope and possibly provide a more dynamic catch. Also, the leader (carrying some traditional protection) could have placed gear along the traverse to protect himself in the event of a fall. Finally, a helmet may have limited the injury to the climber's head. (*Source: Curt Honcharik, Alpine Rescue Team.*)

FALL ONTO TREE BRANCH
Staunton State Park, Tan Corridor

In September, while working on the moves of Ddong Chim! (5.11b), a woman fell partway up this overhanging sport climb. The route begins directly behind a tall conifer, and the woman crashed into a stubby dead branch that points toward the cliff like a dagger. The branch cut a gash in her left buttock that required urgent-care treatment including stitches.

ANALYSIS

Situational awareness is essential, even on well-protected sport climbs. Though it must have seemed unlikely she would hit this branch, awareness of the hazard might have prompted more caution while working the route and taking falls. [*The editor of this publication is intimately familiar with this branch, having swung into it while cleaning the same route; he fended it off with his hand, fortunately suffering only a minor puncture.*] Although conscientious route developers attempt to minimize their impact on cliff-side vegetation, this dead branch should be sawn off in cooperation with the staff of this climber-friendly park. (*Source: Personal accounts.*)

LIGHTNING STRIKE | Multiple Patients
Devils Head, Chicken Head Ranch

June 30 was a normal busy summer Sunday at Devils Head. We started the day on the west side of Chicken Head Ranch to avoid the hot June sun. Toward midday, we moved to the east side, and as usual in the summer, it started to cloud up. We climbed Wishbone Dihedral as the weather started to break down, leaving the rope hanging in case it didn't rain. We had a party of four, and as we waited, two other parties of two came over to the east side of Chicken Head Ranch.

All eight members of the three climbing parties refrained from climbing as the storm brewed to the southwest. As the storm drew closer, but before any rain or hail started, there were several lightning strikes within 500 feet. It was the worst lightning I had experienced in my 45 years of climbing. It was difficult to determine a safe place to be, as there were many tall trees and the crag nearby. Initially, several of us stayed away from the crag, but as the rain, wind, and hail intensified, everyone moved back toward the rock. There were five of us by Wishbone Dihedral, and the other three were about 50 feet to the north by Crystal Key. The lightning hit us at about 3 p.m.

Slowly coming back to my senses, I realized what had happened as I saw two people pass out and fall into the bushes and one other person who was unconscious. I called out to others nearby that they should call 911, thinking they would be unaffected, but they too had been hit as the current fanned out from the top of the crag. I made my way to the phone in my pack and called 911, giving the details of our location and condition to the operator. [*Editor's Note: The author of this report is one of the main route developers at Devils Head and wrote the local guidebook.*] Once I was convinced the operator knew we were on the "back" of the mountain and not on the popular hiking trail to a fire tower, we ended the call.

Everyone was now conscious, but a couple members of the party had obvious issues, especially Sandy, who was standing behind me initially and could not speak. Jody had a bloody nose and was somewhat dazed. The rest of the group were collecting themselves and gathering warm clothes for everyone, as massive hail, rain, and wind continued to pummel the group. Now that it was clear there were people capable of tending to those less well off, I decided to run back to the parking lot to ensure a SAR team could find us. Another member of the group joined me for the 20-minute trip back to the car.

When we reached the parking lot, a Jackson Creek fire truck and one SAR vehicle already had arrived. I confirmed our group's location and the need for at least one stretcher with the SAR team and then raced back up to Chicken Head Ranch with an EMT from Jackson Creek Fire Department. When we reached the group, Sandy was doing a bit better, but had an injured shoulder, and everyone was very cold. When a larger SAR team arrived, Sandy was carried out in a litter, while everyone else hiked out under their own power. Back in the parking lot, we were checked out by para-

ESSENTIALS

LIGHTNING STRIKES
AVOIDANCE AND INJURIES

By Benjamin N. Abo, DO, PMD, FAWM

While being struck by lightning is unlikely for a large portion of the population, it is more of a possibility for climbers due to the locations where we recreate, including ridges, mountaintops, and rock faces. In North America, mountain ranges are common environments for lightning strikes during the summer months. A majority of lightning strikes do not lead to instant death; however, permanent injuries and other issues almost always arise, and furthermore they can lead to secondary accidents from impaired judgment.

TYPES OF STRIKES

Lightning strikes are described by the direction of the strike. A *direct strike* is statistically more physically devastating, with a higher rate of death associated, but much more common are *side flashes* (a.k.a. *side splashes*), where a tree or similar object is struck and the current travels down and "jumps" to a nearby object or person. This is also why groups of people are often struck. A particular risk to climbers are *ground strikes*, where rock is struck and the current travels across or through it. It is critical, also, to understand that lightning can travel quite far and does *not* have to be associated with rain. Thus, the phrase "a bolt from the blue."

PREVENTION

There is no true "safe place" outside when it comes to lightning, other than a well-grounded and protected shelter or vehicle. However, places that are more dangerous include ridgelines, summits, open fields on or near high terrain, boats or open water, near trees at the edge of open water, in the entrance of a shallow cave or overhang, or on the windward side of mountains (where storms come from). Safer locations include dense forest areas away from the tallest tree, low in gullies or draws, or inside deep caves.

In the summer, climbers and mountaineers should aim to be off summits or ridgelines no later than 2 p.m. and ideally by noon. If you are on a vertical face when a thunderstorm approaches, going down is generally the best option, unless by doing so you have to cross more dangerous terrain.

RULES TO LIVE BY: 30-30 FLASH-BANG

When there is an approaching storm, a minimum time span of 30 seconds between flash and thunder indicates that you are a safe distance from the storm. However, you may need more of a gap between flash and bang—i.e., the storm is farther away—to allow adequate time to move to a safer area. In short, start evacuating from exposed locations sooner than you might think is necessary. After a storm passes, wait no less than 30 minutes from the last flash or rumble to resume activities.

It is said that just before an imminent strike, you may feel the hair on the back of your neck or your head rise up. When this occurs, metal objects begin to buzz, or if you are caught by a rapidly approaching storm, assume the safety position—with the term "safety" very loosely used. Find the lowest spot immediately available, spread out if you're in a group, and crouch down with your feet close together and your ears covered. If available, squat on a sleeping or boulder pad, and get away from any metal climbing gear.

COMMON INJURIES FROM STRIKES

Lightning delivers a massive amount of energy in an extremely brief moment. In that instant, electricity travels the path of least resistance, and this is the reason the body's nervous system takes the brunt of both immediate and delayed damage. The impacts include pain and keraunoparalysis, a temporary paralysis, usually of the limbs and associated with pale or mottled skin. Keraunoparalysis can mimic spinal injury and usually resolves after several hours. Vital organs that are affected by electricity include the heart and lungs. It is quite possible for nerves leading to the lungs to be paralyzed. While this is often temporary, lack of breathing (and oxygen) can lead to secondary cardiac arrest or brain injury.

Both direct and indirect strikes can cause other injuries, like those associated with blast injuries from change in air pressure, being thrown into a hard object, or being knocked off of a ledge or stance. It is critical to assess breathing ability after a strike, as collapsed lungs can develop from secondary injuries. Concussions and seizures are also possible.

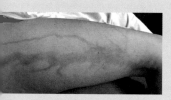

Lichtenberg figures on the skin after a lightning strike. *Michael Bresson*

BURNS

Burns from lightning strikes are not usually a major issue, but wound care needs to be provided to prevent infections. Lightning burns are usually skin-deep and often linear, rather than the entry and exit wounds associated with high-voltage injuries. This is because the electricity flows superficially along the pathway of least resistance. The ferning patterns (Lichtenberg figures) sometimes seen on the skin after strikes are actually not burns and resolve on their own with no permanent issues. Lightning strikes also may cause punctate burns, which are small, circular burns closely spaced together. Check all fingers and toes carefully for these burns.

ALWAYS EVACUATE

Every scenario varies and a plethora of things need to be taken into consideration in terms of how to evacuate, but all people that have experienced a lightning strike should be evaluated medically. Indicators of high-risk injuries include suspected direct hit, loss of consciousness, any nerve, spinal cord, or brain dysfunction, chest pain, shortness of breath, burns to the head, or if the climber is pregnant.

Benjamin N. Abo, DO, PMD, is an EMS and emergency medicine physician in Florida who also practices in international, disaster, and austere medicine, as well as expeditionary filming medicine and safety.

medics and released, except for Jody and Sandy, who were taken via ambulance to nearby hospitals. Sandy ultimately had surgery for a torn ligament in her shoulder, possibly from falling after the lightning strike. Jody had a treatable eye injury.

ANALYSIS
A call to 911 within minutes of the lightning strike and great performance by the first responders helped the injured get to safety relatively quickly. Looking back, it would have been advisable not to move back toward the crag, which stood above the treeline and was hit by the lightning bolt. I had looked for a sheltered spot away from the crag and tall trees, but this was a massive storm with 150 ground strikes in 30 minutes in our area. There really was nowhere safe. I think the biggest takeaway is to stay 50 feet from a lightning target even if it means getting really wet and cold. (*Source: Tod Anderson.*)

GROUND FALL | Rappel Error, No Helmet
Devils Head, Waffle House

On May 27 at approximately 12:30 p.m., a man in his late 20s was rappelling down Bacon Is a Food Group (5.10 sport) and cleaning the draws when he lost his footing and swung over the side of an arête. He swung about 20 feet before slamming headfirst into a rock wall. He didn't have a helmet or a third-hand backup on his rappel. After he hit the wall, he fell at least 10 feet to the snow-packed ground.

A bunch of us rushed over to him. He had a huge, bulging bruise on the left side of his head and blood was coming from his ear. After about seven minutes of drifting in and out of consciousness, he became more alert but was not fully oriented.

We didn't have phone service, but eventually we were able to find a ranger who alerted search and rescue. They sent a helicopter, but it could not land near us due to tree coverage. First responders arrived on foot about an hour after the initial call. The climber was placed in a litter, and a difficult evacuation began through complex terrain, involving multiple agencies. At the trailhead parking, he was transferred to a Flight For Life helicopter. He was talking and responsive when they left. I spoke with his wife the next day, and she told me he had fractured his skull and had brain bleeding/bruising but was not expected to need surgery. (*Source: Brooke Silagy.*)

ANALYSIS
When cleaning a route, it is often safer to remain on belay and be lowered as opposed to cleaning on rappel. On this route, the bolted anchor is off to the side of an angled arête. When the climber lost his footing, the angle of the rappel ropes created a pendulum effect. When a climber lowers to clean a route, they can reduce swing potential by clipping their harness to the belayer's side of the rope with a quickdraw; however, the climber must beware of pulling the belayer off their stance after cleaning the last piece. When rappelling, a fireman's belay from an anchored belayer at the bottom also can help prevent such swings.

It's worth noting the lack of helmet or backup for the rappel. Wearing a helmet likely could have reduced the injury when the climber's head struck the rock, and using a third-hand backup would have kept the injured climber from falling to the ground after losing control of the brake strands. (*Source: The Editors.*)

Red Rib at Castle Rock is about 190 feet high. The standard rappel routes are to the right. In the incident reported here, a party attempted to lower the leader directly from the top with a single rope, which was much too short. *Gary O'Brien*

IDAHO

LOWERING ERROR | Rope Too Short, No Stopper Knot
Castle Rocks State Park, Castle Rock, Southwest Face

On July 21, Dan and Carolyn Morgan were climbing with a group of friends on the southwest face of Castle Rock. The pair were experienced climbers, she with 20 years and he with more than six years of experience. The two were staging an informal climbing and rappelling clinic for their friends. Dan began ascending Red Rib (5.10a), a route that is 190 feet high, with the goal of setting up a top-rope, and Carolyn led Slab Happy (5.9), just left of Red Rib, to set up a practice rappel for the others.

At around 10:10 a.m., Carolyn heard Dan call "take!" and then "lower" to his belayer. She then heard him shout with alarm and watched him free-fall approximately 130 feet to the ground. According to witnesses, the single line used to lower Dan slipped through the belayer's device, causing the uncontrolled fall. No knot was tied in the rope end. Dan fell to a ledge about 20 feet above the base of the climb, and was immediately tended by Carolyn and a friend, who were able to rappel down Slab Happy and traverse over to reach him. Dan was initially found semiconscious with labored breathing, but soon passed away due to multiple traumatic blunt force injuries. (*Sources: Carolyn Morgan, Sarah Carpenter, and Stephen King, ranger at Castle Rocks.*)

ANALYSIS

This incident occurred through a series of overlapping errors. Perhaps most importantly, an atmosphere of relaxed complacency existed within the team of climbers, which may have contributed to errors in judgment, lack of awareness of the scale of the climb, and a clear plan for how the climbers would ascend and descend the route.

Rope too short. This accident could have been avoided by assessing the height of the climb and the length of rope or ropes needed to complete it. A review of the guidebook (and a careful assessment of the cliff itself) would have alerted the climbers that the 70-meter rope they were using was not sufficient for lowering or rappelling directly from the top of Red Rib (190 feet or roughly 58 meters high). A second rope or multiple rappels is required to descend from this climb.

Belay system was not closed, and belayer failed to track the end of the rope. The inexperienced belayer complied with the request to lower and continued until the end of the rope slipped through her Grigri. Had either climber affixed a knot to the end of the rope, the accident would have been prevented. The belayer, whose experience was mainly in gym settings, was unaccustomed to using the entire length of a rope and unquestioningly trusted the more experienced climber to make all the decisions. With more instruction, the belayer would have known to monitor the center of the rope and to alert her climber when the rope was running short.

Lack of clear planning and situational awareness. This incident highlights the importance of the climber clearly communicating a plan with the belayer prior to leaving the ground. The climber was reasonably experienced, but he misinterpreted the height of the route. The goal of climbing Red Rib was to set up a top-rope for others, yet the single 70-meter rope he was using would have been much too short to reach the ground. He then asked to be lowered from the top of the pitch, despite having already climbed nearly 60 meters. (*Sources: Carolyn Morgan, Sarah Carpenter, and the Editors.*)

RAPPEL ERROR | Rappelled off End of Rope
City of Rocks National Reserve, Parking Lot Rock

In the late afternoon of June 22, ranger Stephen King received word that a climber had fallen at Parking Lot Rock. Witnesses and responders said that a 27-year-old female climber was descending from Delay of Game (5.8) when she rappelled off the end of her rope, falling approximately 40 feet and landing on a ledge near the base of the climb. Witnesses stated that her doubled rappel rope was uneven, and there were no knots tied in the ends. The climber suffered an open fracture of her left ankle and an apparent fracture of her left wrist, but was alert and oriented. She was wearing a helmet. The climber was stabilized by EMS personnel and transported from the scene by helicopter. (*Source: Stephen King, ranger at City of Rocks National Reserve and Castle Rocks State Park.*)

ANALYSIS
Researching this climb beforehand would have alerted the climber that rappelling this route requires two ropes or an extra-long single rope. The guidebook (*Bingham*, 2016) states that although the route is 120 feet (36.5 meters) tall, it is possible to lower or rappel with a single 70-meter rope with rope stretch, but they advise to knot the rope ends. (In 2010, a climber fell to the ground when one end of a 70-meter rope passed through his belayer's device as the climber was lowering down this route.) The length of rope this climber used is unknown. Placing the marked center of the rope at the anchor before descending helps to ensure the rope ends are of equal length. If a rope has no accurate center mark, both ends can be lowered simultaneously to keep them even. Whether the rope was too short or the ends were uneven (or both), knotting the rope ends could have been prevented the fall. (*Source: The Editors.*)

RAPPEL ANCHOR FAILURE | Nut and Cam Pulled Out
Black Cliffs, Mid Cliffs Area

On October 8 at about 4 p.m., USAF Tech. Sgt. Peter Kraines (33) and four others were climbing at the Black Cliffs area near Boise. All five were experienced Air Force climbers on orders to conduct climbing training. The five had been climbing since about 11 a.m., and during a final training maneuver they set up a rappel station atop the cliff above More Than I Can Chew (5.9). Sgt. Kraines had assessed the bolted anchor located below the cliff edge and determined that reaching this anchor would create an unsafe situation for the less experienced climbers on the team. The group decided to build an anchor using removable protection at a natural bench above the cliff that offered a more convenient location to assemble and stage the rappel.

An officer who interviewed the team members at the scene described the anchor as a self-equalizing system comprised of two pieces of gear (a number 4 DMM Wallnut and a number 2 DMM Dragon cam) connected by Sterling Power Cord and carabiners, with all placements positioned into vertical cracks between basalt blocks or columns.

Kraines and another climber were clipped to this anchor system as the rappel was being readied. A third climber moved to the bench, rigged his rappel device, and descended to the cliff base. The other climber at the anchor then followed on rappel, with Kraines still secured to the anchor. When this second climber was about

15 feet from the ground, one side of the anchor failed, causing the rappeller to drop a short distance, and then the second piece pulled out, dropping him to the ground. The anchor failure, along with the weight of the climber still on rappel, pulled Kraines from his stance, causing him to fall 53 feet to the ground. The climber on rappel was uninjured, but Kraines sustained traumatic blunt force injuries. His fellow airmen and paramedics performed CPR and a field tracheostomy, but were unable to revive him. (*Sources: Officer Bryan Kindelburger, Ada County Sheriff's Department, and U.S. Air Force Ground Accident Investigation Board Report: Mountain Climbing Mishap, 8 October 2019.*)

Configuration of the rappel anchor that failed at Black Cliffs. A medium cam (missing) was clipped to the cord in the medic's left hand. This setup attempted to equalize the load between the two anchor pieces at the master-point (the lowest carabiner), but when one piece failed, the other was shock-loaded. Load-limiting knots near either side of the master point would minimize extension. *Bryan Kindelberger / Ada County Sheriff's Dept.*

ANALYSIS

All five team members were trained climbers with an advanced emergency medical background. Tech. Sgt. Kraines was trained as a Special Tactics Pararescueman. The team chose to build their anchor above the main cliff. As with many crags formed from basalt, the rock on top of Black Cliff is blockier and more broken than on the cliff face itself. Although the team tested the rock at the anchor site, rock surrounding one of the anchor pieces likely shifted or broke under load, allowing the piece to pull out and propagate force to the other piece, which also pulled out.

The cord they used to construct the anchor was configured in a modified quad, which achieved some equalization between the two pieces of the anchor but did not minimize extension when one piece failed. Thus the remaining piece likely was shock-loaded. Backing up the anchor with at least one additional piece, tying load-limiting knots close to the master point to minimize extension, or choosing an alternative anchor location could have prevented this tragic accident. (*Source: The Editors.*)

KENTUCKY

RAPPEL ERROR | Single-Rope Rappel, Loss of Control
Red River Gorge, Eastern Region

On the evening of July 4, Chief John May (51) of Wolfe County Search and Rescue was rappelling during a rescue operation at Chimney Top Rock in the Red River Gorge. During this single-line rappel, he noted some difficulty in controlling his speed of descent and was unable to come to a complete stop. More than 100 feet from the bottom, when his feet were no longer able to make contact with the cliff, his descent became rapid and the friction of the rope began to burn his hands. Chief May descended through some large trees before making impact with the ground. He suffered rope burns on his left and right fingers, four spinal fractures, a severe concussion, and a torn tendon.

May was rappelling on a 70-meter 10mm dynamic rope using a Mad Rock variable-friction belay/rappel device (the Mad Lock). An optional pin used to add friction to the device was not in place. A 6mm presewn Sterling Auto Block cord, with four wraps, was in place as a backup. Chief May weighed 252 pounds and was carrying an additional 20 pounds of gear, counting his equipment and extra water for the lost hiker. He was wearing a helmet and fingerless leather rescue gloves.

ANALYSIS
Rappelling a single strand of rope requires more friction and greater care with backups than rappelling on two strands. Several weeks after the incident, it was discovered from photos taken during the rescue that the rappel device was unintenionally loaded using the low-friction side of the device. Chief May typically rappelled using the standard, high-friction side of this device for better control. (It was dark at the time, which may have contributed to the mistake.) With the total weight of May and his equipment, the low friction did not adequately control his descent.

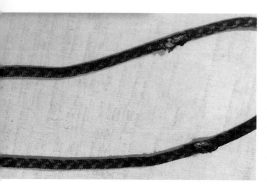

Additionally, it was thought the dynamic rope may have contributed to the loss of control, as the rope would have stretched under load and would have been narrower than its stated 10mm. During the initial part of the rappel, the weight of the rope hanging below May and the weight distributed to his feet on the wall helped him keep control.

Prior to descent, Chief May test-loaded both the rappel device and the autoblock as part of the team's normal safety protocols. Burns on the autoblock cord indicate it engaged but not sufficiently to arrest his fall. The rappel device was not extended, but it did not touch the autoblock during his descent. Based on the burn pattern on his hand, Chief May thinks he may have been clamping down on the autoblock, prevent-

Burns on the rappeller's autoblock cord suggest his backup engaged the rope, but either the friction was insufficient to arrest an uncontrolled descent or the rappeller inadvertently grabbed the autoblock with his brake hand and partially disengaged it. *Wolfe County Search and Rescue*

ing full engagement. It is important to control the brake strand in a way that does not impede the engagement of an autoblock. (*Source: Wolfe County Search and Rescue.*)

RAPPEL ERROR | Uneven Ropes, No Stopper Knots
Red River Gorge, Natural Bridge Region, Emerald City

On August 31, Jarek (27) and his partner were climbing Whiteout (5.8), a two-pitch trad route at Emerald City. After finishing the second pitch, Jarek set up a belay at the anchors, belayed his partner up, and then lowered her to the ground, where she untied and started packing up. He threaded the remaining rope through the anchors and threw it down. He had climbed this route about a month before, so he knew a doubled rope was long enough to make it to the ground. He remembers the rope getting caught on a ledge at the start of the second pitch, but did not pull the rope back up to reset it. His plan was to rappel to the ledge, secure himself to the first-pitch anchors while he made sure the rope reached the ground, and then finish the rappel.

Before Jarek reached the ledge, the end of the rope slipped through his rappel device and he fell approximately 50 feet, tumbling down the blocky portion at the start of the route. He lost consciousness. Wolfe County Search and Rescue responded to the incident and transported Jarek from the crag to an ambulance. He was treated for ankle, foot, wrist, rib, and scapula fractures and a partially collapsed lung. Jarek was not wearing a helmet. (*Sources: Jarek and Wolfe County Search and Rescue.*)

ANALYSIS
Jarek felt sure that both ends of the rope reached the ledge below the second pitch, so he expected to deal with rope management once he was at that point. Since he never made it to the ledge before the end of the rope fed through his device, he suspects the rope was creeping through the anchors as he rappelled, pulling the short end up. (This

is more likely to occur when doing a rappel with two ropes of different diameters tied together.) This accident could have been avoided with stopper knots in the ends of the rope. In addition, with a slower descent, Jarek might have been able to identify the shorter strand before it fed through his device. (*Source: Jarek.*)

FATAL LEAD FALL ON ROCK | Inadequate Knot
Red River Gorge, Muir Valley, Midnight Surf Wall

On the afternoon of September 16, Marty Vogel (59) was working on Baby Face (5.12b) at Midnight Surf in the Muir Valley. For this route, the climber begins on a ledge approximately nine feet above the belayer. They were climbing in a group of three that day, and the belayer had just finished climbing another route when she came over to give Marty a catch. Marty was already on the ledge and tied in, with the route stick-clipped, so she didn't see him tie his knot. Before climbing, Marty indicated to his belayer that his knot was good and he was ready to climb. This was his third attempt on the route that day. The belayer reported that during Marty's ascent he clipped the permadraws on the route and adjusted the rope without any unusual tension or slack.

A bowline tied with the "Yosemite finish."

Marty fell at the eighth bolt of the route. The end of the rope pulled through the tie-in points on his harness and he fell approximately 130 feet, landing 50 feet below the belay station. According to the belayer, she did not feel the expected force from the fall before the rope went slack. The slack rope fell through most of the permadraws and did not have a knot at the end. Marty did not survive the fall.

Wolfe County Search and Rescue inspected the rope and the harness, finding them undamaged and in good condition. (*Source: Wolfe County Search and Rescue.*)

ANALYSIS
According to local climbers, Marty typically climbed with a single bowline with a Yosemite finish (a bowline with the rope's tail threaded back through the knot). Since the belayer was unfamiliar with this knot, she indicated that she was unable to check it on earlier climbs that day. It is most likely that Marty did not complete his knot or did not dress it properly—steps that are particularly important with this knot—allowing it to become untied.

Marty was a beloved member of the local community who regularly volunteered to build and maintain trails, developed new climbing routes, supported gear replacement efforts, and coached young climbers at a local recreation center. He will be missed by all who knew him. (*Sources: Wolfe County Search and Rescue and local climbers.*)

FALL FROM ANCHOR | Lowering Error
Red River Gorge, Muir Valley, Bruise Brothers Wall

On November 8, Jason Miller (42) was cleaning the Offering, a 5.7 sport route at the Bruise Brothers Wall. After tethering to the anchors with slings, Jason threaded a bight of rope through the anchor system, tied a figure-eight on the bight, attached this to his harness with a locking carabiner, and untied his original knot, pulling the tail of the rope through the anchor system. Before detaching his slings from the anchor, Jason had his belayer take out the slack, and he weight-tested the system. It held, and Jason removed his slings. After indicating to his belayer that he was ready to be lowered, Jason felt a jolt and dropped approximately 60 feet to the ground. While falling, Jason remembers positioning his body to land on his side instead of his back.

Wolfe County Search and Rescue responded to the incident and transported Jason from the crag to an ambulance. He was ultimately airlifted to UK hospital in Lexington with a shattered and dislocated right ankle and wrist, a broken right elbow, a fractured pelvis, internal bleeding, and a partially collapsed lung.

According to other climbers in the area, after the fall, the locking carabiner was still attached to Jason's harness and the rope dropped to the ground without any knot in it. Jason was not wearing a helmet. (*Sources: Jason Miller and Wolfe County Search and Rescue.*)

ANALYSIS

While a definitive cause is unknown, it is possible that Jason did not clip the tied bight to his locking carabiner, but instead accidentally clipped another strand of rope within the knot. If this is done with an overhand or a figure-eight on a bight, the system may hold weight temporarily before failing. Consistent vigilance through the entire cleaning process is essential. Testing the knot with a bounce and watching it tighten before untethering from the anchor can further demonstrate that the knot is sufficient. (*Sources: Jason Miller and climbers in the area.*)

MONTANA

LEADER FALL | Huge Broken Hold
Drummond Area, Rattler Gulch, Sidewinder Buttress

On April 22, I (male, 35) was out in Rattler Gulch, climbing an easy stretch of limestone. Since spring in Montana usually means a lot of loose rock from the freeze-thaw cycle, I was testing every hold. I was about 10 to 15 feet above my last piece of protection, a slung tree, and thumped a half-fridge-size block slightly above my head. I had a gut feeling that it was not totally trustworthy, but hitting it showed no movement. I pulled up onto the block and the entire thing crumbled apart, causing a long fall.

Luckily, my belayer was attentive and took in slack rapidly, or I would have hit the deck. My shirt and pants were ripped front and back, with a sharp stick poking through my shirt in two places. My belayer assisted in freeing me from the stick and lowered me safely to the ground. Somewhat dazed, but understanding the danger of rockfall, we moved to a safer area. My feet, arms, right knee, legs, chest, and left hand were all deeply abraded and bloody. As I hobbled over to safety, one last fist-size rock ricocheted off my helmet, cracking it but protecting me from injury.

Shaking with the rush, I sat down. My partner conducted a head to toe assessment. The only other party at the crag came uphill to check on me, bringing water to wash out my wounds and offering their old first-aid kit. They provided me with a pair of ski poles to use on the walk out and assured us they would get the rope and gear I had left on the route. I hobbled down the steep scree slope to the base of the canyon.

ANALYSIS

I was surprised at how easily the large block fell apart after I tested it. This was my first spring on Montana limestone, and most of my experience has been on granite and a little sandstone.

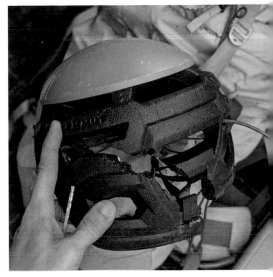

Rockfall *after* the initial accident cracked this helmet, which likely prevented a more serious injury. *Casey Brown*

What went well:
(1) I wore a helmet. This may have saved my life or prevented a severe head injury.
(2) My partner and I had medical and first-aid training. While he's newer to climbing, he is a resident physician. I'm in nursing school and have worked in health care.
(3) My belayer was really attentive and started taking in slack when I fell.
(4) We moved away from the wall after the accident to avoid additional rockfall
(5) I talked honestly about my fears and emotions with my partner after the fall. Doing that helped me to think analytically in a stressful situation, react appropriately, and feel less powerless in the situation.

What went poorly:
(1) I had some tape, toilet paper, and a few knickknacks in an emergency bag in my backpack. I pretended this was a first-aid kit. It was inadequate.
(2) I knew the rock quality was going to be poor, but I decided to climb anyway. I was being careful and testing things, but that isn't always 100 percent.
(3) My belayer wasn't wearing a helmet. His positioning was safe, as I had mentioned he should stay out of the fall line in case I knocked a rock down, but a helmet would have been prudent.
(4) I probably should have stuck to an established route. This area has mostly sport climbs, but I had carried my rack and wanted to show my climbing partner how to place gear, so it seemed logical to just shimmy up an easy alpine-style climb and have a little adventure. (*Source: Casey Brown.*)

THE SHARP END (EPISODE 41): *Casey Brown tells this story in detail in "A Montana Mishap (Why More Leaders Should Wear Helmets)" on the Sharp End podcast.*

RIDGE COLLAPSE IN 4TH-CLASS TERRAIN
Absaroka Range, Mt. Cowen

On the morning of July 14, at 4:30 a.m., Jackson Negri (25), Travis Swanson (33), and Will Hitchcock (29) began hiking from the East Mill Creek trailhead with the intention of group soloing Mt. Cowen via the northeast arête. This route is a prominent granitic ridge that runs for about 1,000 vertical feet directly to the 11,212-foot summit; it is mostly 4th-class terrain with a few 5.6 crux sections. Due to the perceived low risk and their plan to solo the route and then walk off the southwest side of the mountain, the three climbers decided not to take gear (rope, harness, or helmets). They did have a light medical kit, cellphones, a handheld radio, and a Garmin inReach.

The day was almost perfectly clear when the group reached the start of the route and began climbing. At 10:48 a.m., they were roughly halfway up. Negri was about 30 feet in front of the others when he heard a scream from Swanson and saw rockfall, including a car-size boulder, tumbling into the Strawberry Creek drainage to the north. Based on the location of the rockfall, it seems the climbers were standing on

The northeast arête of Mt. Cowen from the air, showing the couloir where two climbers landed after a portion of the ridge collapsed. (A) Origin of the rockfall and last known position of the two climbers. (B) Location of injured climber. (C) Approximate location of second climber. (D) Rockfall swept out the gully to the north here. *Ladean McKittrick*

a large section of the ridge when it collapsed underneath them. Negri began downclimbing the route and found no sign of Swanson or Hitchcock. At 10:51 a.m., he called 911 via his cellphone, and Gallatin County Search and Rescue (GCSAR) was dispatched shortly afterward.

Negri deduced that his partners had fallen into a couloir that parallels the ridge. In order to access the couloir, Negri continued to downclimb their route to a ledge that led into the couloir. He then was able to look up the couloir, and from this vantage point he could see Hitchcock lying face-first in the snow with dark blood around his head. Negri found Hitchcock with numerous severe injuries; he was responsive to pain but not able to speak. He was partially buried in snow and pinned under a large boulder that had prevented him from continuing to fall down the 45° to 50° slope. Negri bandaged Hitchcock with his medical kit and began excavating a snow platform while simultaneously digging Hitchcock out from under the boulder and keeping him from sliding down the couloir.

Six members of GCSAR responded using two separate helicopters, with the first team making visual contact with the climbing party at approximately 12:30 p.m. At 12:50 p.m. Negri looked down the couloir and identified Swan-

continued on page 77...

ESSENTIALS

FIRST-AID KITS
NOT JUST WHAT, BUT ALSO WHY

By Corey Winstead

Climbers are naturally detail oriented. We compare carabiner weights, argue over gates in or gates out, and research beta down to which way to hold that crimp rail on the third pitch. This level of scrutiny, and the intention that goes into it, makes us more successful on our objectives and helps us manage risk. This is an article about first-aid kits, but let's not dive right into what to include in a kit. Instead, let's consider how to think about what you want to carry, and the answers may reveal themselves.

CONSIDER YOUR OBJECTIVE

We carry first-aid kits to mitigate risk. As climbers, whether placing gear or investigating a snowpack or practicing self-rescue, we learn about risks, consider them, and employ strategies to fit them into our own acceptable-risk paradigm. Packing a first-aid kit should be no different.

Risk is a product of probability and severity. The *probability* or likelihood that an event will come to pass is both objective and subjective. Rockfall risk in the alpine is fairly objective, though the likelihood might change depending on whether there are other climbers above you, time of day, season, etc. The risk of falling on a route is more subjective, and often depends largely upon the chosen objective and your individual skill, comfort, and strength. Severity is related to the outcome should the event in question occur. For example, the severity of being hit by rockfall is generally more significant than falling on top-rope.

The items in your first-aid kit can help you manage the severity of an event, while your good decisions up to that point will have the greatest effect on probability.

RISK/BENEFIT

It would be naïve to believe that packing a first-aid kit for a climbing day has only benefits and no costs. Putting together a kit takes time, effort, and financial resources. Carrying a kit on a big climb or a long day in the alpine expends additional energy. If your kit is so large that it slows you down, it may even increase the likelihood of certain hazards.

Thus, the consideration of what to pack in a first-aid kit must include not only probability and severity of various events, but also the utility of each item in your kit. Put another way, the utility of the items is directly related to whether they can affect the eventual outcome of an incident. For example, you will need almost a full roll of one-inch athletic tape to properly tape an ankle, but being able to do so might allow you to self-evacuate in the backcountry, whereas without it you might be calling for help. Conversely, if you sprain an ankle at a roadside crag, you will be able to hobble back to the car regardless of whether you have the tape.

THE GOODS

The severity/likelihood chart below lists some common first-aid and survival kit items and the rationale for carrying them. This graph is a good place to start when considering the risks and needs for your objectives. Note that fields for "not severe/ unlikely" and "severe/likely" have been omitted, as it stands to reason that events that are both inconsequential and unlikely do not need to be planned for, and that we rarely knowingly venture into environments where severe consequences are likely.

SEVERE – UNLIKELY	NOT SEVERE – LIKELY
• Extremity hemorrhage – tourniquet • Major catastrophe – inReach, phone, PLB • Unplanned night out – shelter, stove, water purification • Sprained ankle/broken bone – SAM splint, tape • Anaphylactic reaction – epinephrine	• Blister – tape, blister bandage • Splinter – tweezers • Sunburn – sunscreen/lip balm • Hangnail – fingernail clippers • Sore muscles – NSAIDs • Minor laceration – gauze • Cold hands – hand warmers

Another way to consider first-aid and survival kit contents is the PAWS acronym:

Prevention/Procedures – knife, water purification tablets, athletic tape, lip balm/ sunscreen

Analgesics/Antibiotics/Anaphylaxis – ibuprofen, acetaminophen, diphenhydr-amine, loperamide, antacid, bacitracin ointment, epinephrine

Wound Care – hemostatic gauze, blister bandage/tape, assorted gauze (2x2, 3x3, etc.), latex-free gloves, adhesive bandages, alcohol prep pad, antiseptic wipes

Survival – whistle, survival blanket, lighter, communication device

PRACTICAL DETAILS

- Every item on the lists above requires knowledge and experience to use. Wilderness medicine training will prepare you to anticipate risks and to react appropriately in an emergency.
- While your first-aid kit may help you stabilize a severe injury, the definitive action for most major accidents will be prompt evacuation to a hospital. Know which communication methods will work where you are going and plan ahead. Emergency devices that allow two-way communication will speed emergency response.
- Pack only what you're willing to carry. Your kit doesn't do you any good sitting in the car.
- Items expire, time takes its toll. Check your kit regularly to make sure it's still functioning and still meets your needs.

BOTTOM LINE

Your first-aid kit is more than just tape and gloves. Pack it with intention and adapt it to each objective the same way you would the gear on your harness or the shoes on your feet.

Corey Winstead is a wilderness medicine instructor and physician assistant student living in Asheville, N.C. He is also the assistant chief of the Appalachian Mountain Rescue Team.

...continued from page 74

son's body wedged in a slot that ran along the edge of the couloir. The first team of responders arrived and began assisting Hitchcock at 1:08 p.m. They short-hauled him at 1:46 p.m. to an awaiting air ambulance stationed near the highway. The second GCSAR team accessed Swanson at 2 p.m. but found him deceased due to head trauma.

Hitchcock suffered a fractured C2 vertebra, a chipped left femur, traumatic brain injury, degloving of his scalp, and numerous lacerations. He received several surgeries over the course of the next few months and is making a full recovery. Travis Swanson's passing has left a hole in the hearts of many.

ANALYSIS

Negri, Hitchcock, and Swanson were very active and well-trained members of Gallatin County Search and Rescue. Negri's good decision-making, his knowledge of first aid, and his ability dig out Hitchcock were crucial in his partner's rescue. Although the route was well within their abilities, any travel in fourth-class terrain brings the risk of loose rock and includes areas of "no fall" terrain. Choose appropriate footwear, be vigilant for loose rock, and have the appropriate gear (helmet, harness) for any terrain you might encounter. (*Source: Gallatin County Search and Rescue.*)

FALL ON ICE | Inadequate Gear, Failure to Self-Arrest
Granite Peak, Granite Glacier

On July 19, two male climbers (ages 24 and 25) ascended the east ridge of Granite Peak (ca. 12,800 feet), summiting at 1:30 a.m on June 20. They became disoriented while attempting to descend in the dark and decided to bivy a few hundred meters to the east of the summit and continue in the morning. At sunrise, they began to rappel down the north face, and after 12 rappels they reached the Granite Glacier. Equipped with only running shoes and one ice axe each, they tried to downclimb the 50-degree-plus slope of the glacier. After 25 feet, the first climber lost his footing, was unable to self-arrest, and slid about 75 feet before stopping, uninjured, when he ran into a rock field. His partner fell shortly afterward and also was unable to self-arrest, sliding about 450 feet into a large rock platform and sustaining lacerations and bruising to his ankles. The two climbers activated the SOS function on their personal locator beacon, and Gallatin County Search and Rescue responded within two hours, short-hauling the injured climber off the mountain.

ANALYSIS

The climbers in this incident made a good decision in delaying their descent, and they were prepared for an overnight stay on the mountain. They had not planned to descend via the glacier, so they did not have the equipment needed to successfully navigate this terrain (crampons or even Microspikes), and their inability to self-arrest on the icy glacier directly led to the accidents and associated injuries. The injured climber was lucky to escape a slide of this length with relatively minor injuries and no fractures. (*Sources: Gallatin County Search and Rescue and the Editors.*)

UNROPED FALLS IN CLASS III/IV TERRAIN
Beartooth Mountains, Granite Peak, Southwest Ramp

Aerial view of Granite Peak's southwest side. (A1) Approximate site of August 24 fall from fourth-class terrain. (A2) Patient's location after fall. (B1) Site of August 20 fall in snow couloir. (B2) Patient's location after fall. *Joe Wagner*

Two falls occurred within the same week in August on the Southwest Ramp route of Granite Peak, the highest point in Montana. On August 20, a 50-year-old female climber slipped on a section of snow in the couloir portion of the route and was unable to self-arrest. She tumbled approximately 300 feet through rocky terrain and suffered a severe head injury along with fractures to an arm and leg. Her partner, along with help from another party, was able to contact search and rescue, and the injured climber was short-hauled from the mountain and transferred to a local hospital.

On August 24, a 65-year-old male climber fell approximately 50 to 100 feet after losing his footing in fourth-class terrain about 200 feet below the summit. At this point on the climb, the couloir ends and the route-finding becomes more challenging; the terrain can go from third-to fourth-class very quickly if you get off-route. The climber sustained extensive injuries, and efforts by his son (33) and other climbers to resuscitate him were unsuccessful.

ANALYSIS

Although the Southwest Ramp (sometimes called the Southwest Couloir) is climb-able without a rope, many trip reports recommend carrying one for use by parties who are uncomfortable in exposed class III and IV terrain and to allow for an easier descent via rappel. See "Know the Ropes: Safer 4th Class" in Accidents 2018 for more ideas on moving safely and efficiently through such terrain. (*Sources: Gallatin County Search and Rescue and the Editors.*)

NEW HAMPSHIRE

FALL ON ROCK | Long Runout, Inadequate Protection
Cannon Cliff, Moby Grape

At 11:30 a.m. on September 15, Liam Kirkpatrick (20) and his partner were climbing Moby Grape (8 pitches, 5.8 PG-13) on Cannon Cliff. The 5.7 fifth pitch of this route wanders, and from the traditional belay stance it is not possible to see the leader. Kirkpatrick took an unexpected fall and dislocated his elbow. (At the time, he believed he had broken his arm.) He communicated to his partner, who began lowering him. Then Kirkpatrick dropped again—another 30 to 45 feet. Due to the ensuing confusion, neither is sure if the slack resulted from a piece pulling or if the rope had snagged over the many bushes on the wandering, slabby pitch and suddenly popped free.

In the course of the second fall, Kirkpatrick landed on the ledge near his partner. In addition to the dislocated elbow, Kirkpatrick suffered an acetabular hip fracture and seven fractured vertebrae. Members of New Hampshire Fish and Game, Pemigewasset Search and Rescue, and Mountain Rescue Service took the nearby ski-resort tram to the top of the cliff to respond, and several parties lower on the route climbed up to the injured party. A New Hampshire National Guard Black Hawk helicopter lowered a guardsman and litter, retrieved Kirkpatrick, and transferred him to Dartmouth Hitchcock Medical Center. This was the first helicopter pick-off of an injured climber on technical terrain in New Hampshire. (*Sources: New Hampshire Fish and Game Department, Venkata Damaraju, Liam Kirkpatrick, and the Editors.*)

ANALYSIS

Cannon is a very large alpine cliff with loose rock, ledges, wetness, and vegetation. Even the most popular routes have unavoidable runouts and sections where falls will have serious consequences. The fifth pitch of Moby Grape is not difficult but is difficult to protect. The low angle makes for especially dangerous terrain in the event of a fall. Though Kirkpatrick—an experienced climber for whom Moby Grape felt comfortable—can't remember why he fell, it is probable he slipped on the pitch's hardest move, ascending a short slab with poor protection. In run-out terrain, the main thing protecting the leader is his or her movement skills. Concentration, careful movement, and testing holds are paramount, as is striving to ensure that every piece is solid and extended where necessary to minimize shifting. (*Source: The Editors.*)

GROUND FALL | Inadequate Protection
Franconia Notch, Echo Crag

On August 24, at Echo Crag, Lizzy Ragan (24) fell while climbing Avalanche (5.7), a single-pitch trad route. Lizzy was reported to be comfortable leading 5.10 sport, but was new to leading traditionally protected routes.

According to her partner on the climb, "It was intended to be a nice and easy, mellow cragging day, and we were just starting our warm-up climbs." Lizzy had successfully led a nearby 5.6 trad route and had just followed Avalanche before deciding to attempt the lead.

Lizzy placed a small cam (purple Metolius 0) as her first piece and knew that she needed to place something larger. However, her foot slipped before she could get a larger piece in. As her fall loaded the small cam, the piece popped, throwing her sideways. In all, she fell about 10 to 15 feet, landing on a small set of stone stairs and sustaining massive damage to her spine. Lizzy was wearing a helmet, which may have prevented a fatal injury.

The community of climbers at the crag, several of whom had wilderness first responder and first-aid training, quickly got Lizzy stabilized and called for a rescue. She was carried out on a litter and loaded for a helicopter evacuation. She reached

Dartmouth Hitchcock Medical Center within two hours of the fall.

Lizzy sustained a serious spinal cord injury to her C1–2 and T4–5 vertebrae and no longer has use of her legs. She underwent surgery to stabilize her condition and began long-term rehabilitation.

ANALYSIS

Lizzy was actively training in trad climbing with qualified and experienced partners. She was leading a route that she was familiar with and within her technical ability.

Placing solid trad gear near the start of a climb is critical to avoid a ground fall. Small cams, especially in less than ideal placements, often will not hold large fall forces. In this case, the uneven terrain below the climb caused a relatively modest fall to have catastrophic consequences. Lizzy attests that, had she not placed the first piece (the one that popped under load), she perhaps would not have flipped upside down and would have hit the ground with her feet instead of injuring her spine. (*Sources: Online accounts from Lizzy Ragan and Alice Chiang.*)

FALL ON ROCK | Inexperienced Belayer
Rumney, Armed and Dangerous Area

On June 22, George (30) was leading and Steff (30) was belaying on Toxic Gumbo, a 5.8 sport climb on the left side of Main Cliff at Rumney. On a low-angled slab above an overhang, and while out of sight to the belayer, George unexpectedly fell.

This was Steff's first time lead belaying, and the instruction she had received prior to the climb was that she would feel a strong jerk in the event of a fall. When George fell on the slab, the overhang prevented her from seeing him, and because of the low angle (and likely some rope drag) his slide pulled up the rope gradually. Steff believed George was either tugging on the rope to clip or was climbing quickly on easy terrain, and so she payed out slack. She continued to do so until he dropped into her field of vision. After a leader fall of about 30 feet, she applied the belay and stopped his fall. (*Source: Stephanie Duhem.*)

ANALYSIS

Fortunately, George suffered only minor abrasions, but this accident brings up issues important to climbers making the transition to outdoor crags. The instruction Steff received in a climbing gym led her to expect a sharp upward yank with a leader fall. In this instance, the impact she felt was much less than expected, and so she mistakenly fed out rope.

In complicated natural terrain and difficult conditions, clear communication is essential. The leader can call for "slack" or "clipping" to help the belayer know to feed out a little more rope. (George had stopped yelling commands because the cliff was crowded and noisy that day.) The leader can call "watch me" before a dicey move to increase the belayer's vigilance, and always should yell "falling" to alert them to catch a fall.

With a novice belayer, it might have been wiser for the experienced leader to choose a climb having a clear line of sight, with minimal chance of a leader fall, and to have a person backing up and instructing the belayer. (*Sources: Stephanie Duhem and the Editors.*)

LEAD FALL ONTO LEDGE | Off-Route, Inadequate Protection
Cathedral Ledge, Barber Wall

On September 8, Sean Goodrich (45) and his partner planned on climbing Funhouse to Upper Refuse, the classic moderate link-up on Cathedral Ledge. After finishing Funhouse (5.7), the pair eyed what they thought to be Upper Refuse (5.5), a right-leaning corner above a big ledge. In reality, they were looking at Retaliation (5.9), a route notorious for its tricky to-protect crux, one buttress to the left of Refuse.

From the ledge below, Retaliation (left) and Upper Refuse (right) follow similar right-trending ramps, but the former is a much more difficult climb. *Alex Smith (left) and Ladd Raine*

Goodrich led up Retaliation's initial ramp, placing sparse protection because of the easy climbing. When he got to the crux, he was run-out. At this point, he fell approximately 25 feet. He hit his left side against the wall and landed on the mid-height ledge that separates Retaliation from Upper Refuse. No gear blew, but his pieces were widely separated and there was some slack in the belay. He had fallen backward, possibly due to the rope catching his feet, and landed on his back, hitting his head. He was awake, alert, and in a lot of pain.

The belayer lowered Goodrich to a small ledge above the base of the climb and called 911. Responders from Bartlett Jackson Medical Service, North Conway Fire Department, and Mountain Rescue Service quickly reached the accident scene by way of the summit road. Nearby climbers also came to Goodrich's aid and were able to get the climber into a litter and lower him the remaining 25 feet to the base of the climb. The litter was then carried across the exposed area below the climb and up to the summit area. He was air evacuated to Maine Medical in Portland. He suffered serious injuries consisting of a torn aorta, fractures in his pelvis, back, ribs, neck, and arm, and a concussion.

ANALYSIS

Goodrich was coming off an injury but expected to be able to climb Upper Refuse without difficulty. Just before the fall, a nearby climber heard him say to his belayer, "This feels hard for 5.5." Retaliation and Upper Refuse share many distinguishing features, and it is not hard to imagine mistaking one route for the other; both start in the same general area, and both start with a right-trending ramp. However, carefully reading the route descriptions shows that Upper Refuse includes a chimney, gully, and tree ledge features, while Retaliation follows a single, prominent right-trending crack system the whole way.

Route-finding on traditional climbs is an important skill that takes experience to develop. Read guidebooks and websites (including the comments) for descriptions of a route new to you. Continually check the route description against what you find as you progress up the route. If you are in doubt, you can always stop, re-evaluate, and consider downclimbing, lowering, or rappelling. If you choose to "go for it," make sure to place solid protection before proceeding into unknown terrain. Protecting an easy section of a climb sometimes seems like a chore, but it's an important one. (*Sources: Tyler Smith, Sean Björnsson, and the Editors.*)

FATAL FALL ON SNOW | Climbing Alone, Failure to Self-Arrest
Mt. Washington, Huntington Ravine

On February 10, Jeremy Ullmann, 37, was attempting to solo climb Central Gully, an easy snow and ice climb in Huntington Ravine. His partner had turned back earlier in the day. After Ullmann was reported overdue at 4:45 p.m., search and rescue teams and U.S. Forest Service snow rangers assembled to search the terrain near the route. His body was found in the Fan, a rocky area approximately 300 feet below the climb, at 7:45 p.m. He was equipped with crampons and two ice axes and had attempted to self-arrest. (*Source: Mt. Washington Avalanche Center.*)

ANALYSIS
On the day of the incident, temperatures had dropped to around 0°F on the mountain following several days of above-freezing temperature and rain. According to the Mt. Washington Avalanche Center, very icy conditions had developed. Although the slope angle where Ullmann fell was only 35 degrees, self-arrest would have been very difficult in these conditions.

When traveling over icy terrain, even on relatively low-angle ground, careful movement and use of crampons is more important than self-arrest, which may not be successful. Particular care must be taken to avoid catching one's crampon points in clothing or straps—this climber's crampon straps had not been trimmed. An anchored belayer could have stopped this fall, but it is not unusual to climb this slope without a belay. According to the Mt. Washington Avalanche Center report, the patient's injuries might have been reduced by wearing the helmet that he carried on his pack, but they likely still would have been fatal because of the high-speed slide into rocks. (*Source: The Editors.*)

SKIING FALL INTO WATERFALL HOLE
Mt. Washington, Tuckerman Ravine

At 1:58 p.m. on April 22, a skier fell over the Tuckerman Ravine headwall and into one of several holes in the snowpack that frequently open in this area in the spring, caused by waterfalls flowing off rock walls. Partners and bystanders quickly initiated rescue efforts and called 911 for emergency response. A beacon search was started. At 2:18 p.m., after 20 minutes out of view of the rescuers, the subject climbed out of a different hole in the snow. He had lost his skis, poles, and pack.

The subject was alert, oriented, and able to walk but in pain from several impacts during the fall. He was also cold and wet after spending most of the 20 minutes maneuvering through very cold flowing water. The rescue party quickly changed his clothes to drier ones. They wrapped him in a sleeping bag and briefly transported him in a rescue litter obtained from the nearby Connection Cache of emergency supplies. Hoping to warm the subject, the rescue party then helped him walk down toward Hermit Lake, below Tuckerman Ravine.

Meanwhile, U.S. Forest Service snow rangers were notified of the incident by emergency dispatchers. They traveled to Hermit Lake with urgency, aware that similar accidents in Tuckerman have been fatal. They met the patient and rescue party at 3:20 p.m., on their way down to Hermit Lake. The subject was transported to Pinkham Notch via snowcat and released to the care of friends.

A fallen skier is helped down Tuckerman Ravine after falling over the rocky headwall and into a crevasse-like hole. The glissade tracks just right of the group lead almost directly to the accident site. *USFS Snow Ranger Ryan Matz*

ANALYSIS

As winter turns rapidly to spring, a number of hazards become prevalent in the steep terrain of the Presidential Range—and particularly the Headwall area of Tuckerman Ravine. Waterfall holes, glide cracks or crevasses, moats around cliffs and rocks, and other deep holes open as the thick snowpack melts. These holes present severe terrain traps in the event of a fall. They also can be very difficult to escape or be rescued from (and dangerous to rescuers), and with significant amounts of cold water often flowing inside, a fall into one of these holes can quickly lead to hypothermia. Such accidents have resulted in several fatalities in Tuckerman Ravine. Had the subject, who was a strong athlete and a climber, been unable to self-extricate from the waterfall hole, the outcome could have been far worse.

The subject's partners and bystanders had sufficient dry clothing and emergency supplies to provide proper care for the patient. Rescuers knew that a litter and hypothermia wrap materials were available in the nearby Connection Cache and used them. All individuals on the scene had avalanche rescue gear. This group's timely and appropriate action is commendable. (*Source: Mt. Washington Avalanche Center.*)

NEW MEXICO

RAPPEL ANCHOR FAILURE
Sandia Mountains, Chimney Canyon

On July 13, two men and a woman went to Chimney Canyon in the Sandias, planning to rappel the 140-foot route Skinwalker (5.10+) in order to preview gear placements on the climb. The woman went to the base of the crag while the two others went to the top and created a three-piece rock anchor in granite, using one number 3 Camalot and two

Omega Pacific Link Cams that were equalized with a 240cm Dyneema sling. A single static rope was employed for the rappel, and a Grigri was used as the descent device.

They had brought a dog to the top of the crag, and one of the climbers left the anchor station to make sure the dog was tied up. As he left the anchor, he looked back and saw that his friend, Garon Coriz, 33, was placing a 60-liter backpack under the area of the anchor in an effort to protect the rope and anchor material against abrasion. Feeling comfortable that his friend was capable of managing the rappel, and that both of them had been confident in the anchor they had set, the climber went to attend to the dog.

The woman at the base also left to help with the dog but stated that she saw the rappel rope being thrown and that, since it became entangled, it was being pulled back up to the top of the cliff at the time she left the base. Approximately 15 minutes later, the climber heard a scream and returned to the anchor, where he saw that all of the gear and the rope were gone. Coriz did not survive the 140-foot fall. The accident was unwitnessed.

ANALYSIS

The Albuquerque Mountain Rescue team investigated the rope and the anchor components, which were found at the bottom of the climb. The Grigri was clipped to Coriz's harness, and the rope was correctly installed in the device for rappelling. The investigators found that the Grigri was approximately eight feet from the anchor pieces on the ground. (A different report stated this distance was only four feet.) They also found that the Link Cams were damaged and opened wider than their normal stopping point, indicating they had pulled out under high force.

It is speculated that Coriz may have started the rappel but then returned to the anchor for some reason, without pulling rope through the Grigri to take up the eight feet (or four feet) of slack that accumulated. A slip or fall with slack in the rappel rope could cause a fall factor as high as 1. With a static rope, this would generate a very significant impact force on the anchor.

Although all of the cams used in this anchor are designed to resist pulling out against very high forces, this is only true in good placements in solid rock. In this case, the pack that was positioned under the rope and anchor (presumably to provide edge protection) likely shifted the position and vector of pull on one or all of the cams immediately prior to the fall. It's also possible that the rock around the anchor may have been weaker than it appeared.

Once rock anchors have been placed, they should remain in their intended direction and should not be used after movement without further inspection and/or appropriate readjustment. In addition, static ropes can create high impact forces on anchors as well as the climber—they should never be shock loaded. Pre-equalized anchors are never truly equalized, and sequential failure of rock anchors can happen. Lastly, maintain tension in the rope at all times during a rappel (or while standing at a belay anchor); avoid creating slack that can result in higher than expected impact forces in the event of a slip or fall.

Dr. Garon Coriz was a physician from Albuquerque and Kewa Pueblo, and was an advocate for Bears Ears National Monument and Native American rights. He will be greatly missed. (Source: *James Marc Beverly, Ph.D., IFMGA guide.*)

NEW YORK

SHAWANGUNKS ANNUAL SUMMARY
Mohonk Preserve

In 2019 there were 22 reported climbing-related accidents on the Mohonk Preserve. Injuries sustained during these accidents included: three head injuries, one fractured jaw, one spinal fracture, one pelvis fracture, two long bone fractures, and a number of ankle, wrist, shoulder, and hand injuries. Eleven accidents required technical rescue, including four high-angle rescues. Four uninjured climbers were rescued after becoming stranded, either on rappel or while ascending.

One injured climber was attempting to pinkpoint Higher Stannard (5.9) in the Trapps after preplacing gear while on rappel. Just below the first-pitch crux, the climber fell. The highest preplaced gear pulled, and the climber fell to the ground. The climber suffered multiple traumatic injuries. This was one of several accidents in the Gunks involving gear "failure"—generally gear pulling out of the rock.

On two separate occasions, climbers were rescued when an attempt to rappel in the Near Trapps left them stranded. The Fat City rappel (200 feet) requires two 70-meter ropes to reach the ground. This rappel is notorious for leaving climbers dangling in midair when attempting to descend with a single rope. In one of the incidents, the climber had no stopper knots below the belay device and less than 10 inches of rope to hold onto. Mohonk Preserve rangers performed pick-off rescues for each incident and returned the climbers safely to the ground.

Another stranding incident began with two climbers attempting to climb Loose Goose (5.6) in the Near Trapps. On the second pitch, the leader went off-route and was unable to continue. The leader was approximately 50 feet above and 60 feet left of their second on a small ledge, and struggling with significant rope drag. The leader asked the second to secure themself to a tree with a sling and untie from the rope system so the leader could descend. However, the leader then realized there were no significant anchor options and became stranded. With darkness arriving, climbers on the ground called 911, and Mohonk rangers rescued the stranded party.

Rockfall was involved in one reported climbing accident, and a belayer being pulled into the wall accounted for another.

There were three bouldering accidents that occurred after poor spotting resulted in uncontrolled falls. Injuries sustained included fractured lower extremities, lacerations, and head injuries. At least one bouldering accident resulted from the climber completing a highball problem (50 feet) and then slipping on the descent.

ANALYSIS
Several of these incidents could have been avoided if those involved had the ability to self-rescue. In addition, several were caused because climbers did not properly prepare for descents longer than a single-rope rappel. Knowledge of self-rescue and understanding descent options and requirements by carefully consulting route descriptions would have prevented many of the technical rescues during the past year. (*Sources: Andrew Bajardi, Chief Ranger, Mohonk Preserve, and the Editors.*)

NORTH CAROLINA

RAPPEL ERROR | Inadequate Equipment, Removed Backup
Pisgah National Forest, Looking Glass Rock, South Side

Jed (42) and I (28) climbed frequently at Looking Glass Rock, specifically the South Side area. On February 2, a sunny, bluebird day, we had planned to get on a different route and carried only one 60-meter rope with us. However, when we passed Dinkus Dog (5.10b) and saw that it was available, we decided to give it a go, as it was also on our tick list. We climbed the two pitches of Dinkus Dog to the top, alternating leads. We are both comfortable leading 5.10 trad and had no issues climbing the route.

We knew we needed two ropes to rappel from the anchors straight to the ground, but also knew there were convoluted rappel options to get down with one rope. A comment on Mountain Project mentioned a solid tree about halfway up and to the left of the route, and our analysis from the ground confirmed this was a viable option.

Once we were at the top, we decided to rappel to the tree and set up a sling anchor there to rappel to the ground. As it was a slightly diagonal first rappel to the tree, we placed a cam about 20 feet to the left of the anchors as a directional, so the rappel line would run straight down to the tree. The plan was that Jed would rappel first to set up the lower anchor. When it was my turn, I could remove the cam and then follow the diagonal rope to his anchor at the tree. We typically simul-rappel, as we are similar in weight, but did not this time. We always tie knots in the ends of our rope, use an ATC with an extension, and use a prusik backup. This rappel was no exception.

While our cam placement made the rappel safer from a directional standpoint, it left Jed about three feet short of the tree. I shouted down for him to place a cam and anchor himself to it so I could remove the directional up top and thus release enough rope for him to safely reach the tree. However, he shouted back that he had the situation under control, as he was able to unweight the rope using a small shelf for his feet. His plan was to extend his belay device with a long sling. However, in a lapse in judgment, he also removed his prusik and untied the knots from the ends of the rope, thinking he would need as much rope as possible to reach the tree. Due to the new extension, he couldn't easily grab the brake strands of the rappel rope. He apparently either lost his balance or weighted the rappel system expecting the back-ups he had removed to hold him. The ends of the rope passed through his device, and I watched him free-fall more than 100 feet to the ground.

I thought that he had died and started screaming, alerting other climbers in the area. I also immediately dialed 911 and set a rescue in motion. An amazing community of climbers, including an ER nurse who was first on the scene, was able to stabilize Jed at the bottom. He hit ledges, trees, and brush on the way down and landed on dirt as opposed to the slab. He never lost consciousness and recalls "actively falling." He was wearing a helmet.

Once I heard he did not appear to have life-threatening injuries, I pulled up the rope and saw the knots we had tied in the ends were no longer there. I lowered one end to a climber below, and he tied on a second rope, which I pulled up and then was able to make a single rappel to the bottom. Upon assessing that Jed had no damage to his spine, we carried him from the base of the cliff toward Slick Rock Trail, where we met a rescue team who helped carry him the rest of the way out in a litter. He was airlifted to Mission Trauma Center in Asheville. Miraculously, he sustained only three broken ribs, broken spinous processes, a ruptured right Achilles tendon, and abrasions down his right side.

Jed, the climber in the Looking Glass accident, is seen here looking for a cam placement to establish a temporary directional piece for a diagonal rappel. This turned out to leave him short of rope to reach the next rappel anchor, with serious consequences. *Amanda Ellis*

ANALYSIS

The accident happened because of a lapse in judgment and the removal of rappel safety backups. It was entirely preventable. Similar accidents can be avoided by never removing these backups and carrying two ropes where necessary to rappel as opposed to attempting convoluted rappel options. [Editor's Note: An additional consideration is that the climber may have weighted the system without having his hand on the brake strands of the rappel, trusting his third-hand backup to hold him. Although resting on a prusik or autoblock is often useful for cleaning gear or untangling rope while rappelling, it's safest to do with the rappel ropes held in one's hand or otherwise secured.] (Source: Amanda Ellis.)

BOULDERING FALL | Dislocated Ankle on Pad
Rumbling Bald

On March 28, Noah Cleveland (20), Ben Rader (19), Carson Yates (19), and I (22) went to Rumbling Bald to boulder. Ben and I were familiar with the area, and our plan was to introduce Noah and Carson to bouldering outdoors, so we focused on moderate problems. The weather was warm and clear. After climbing one problem, I got on Short Crack (V2). The landing area was flat, with no rocks or roots, and we placed several crash pads. Because the problem was short, I decided not to top out. Instead I dropped about four to five feet onto a crash pad, but I landed on the outside of my right foot, dislocating the ankle. Ben was able to support my shoulders when I dropped, so my head never hit the pad. I was able to reduce the dislocation and elevate it on a log while the rest of the group finished a couple more problems, then I walked out slowly.

The swelling really kicked in on the drive home. Later that night, I was unable to support my weight and could not walk for the next day and a half. I visited an orthopedic specialist who took an X-ray and confirmed that I had dislocated and sprained the ankle. It took me six months to fully recover. (Source: Anna Marie Alewine.)

ANALYSIS

One takeaway from this incident is that you don't have to be climbing a big or difficult objective to get into trouble. In my case, I was doing an easy boulder problem with a flat, well-padded landing zone. You can "play it safe" and still get hurt. Assess the landing area before climbing and make a mental image of where you plan to land. Though not a factor in this accident, careful pad placement can prevent landing on an edge of a pad, as can adjusting crash pads to follow a climber as she moves, especially on problems that traverse. (*Sources: Anna Marie Alewine and the Editors.*)

FALL ON ROCK | Rope Behind Leg, No Helmet
Pilot Mountain State Park, The Parking Lot

During the afternoon of May 6, ranger J. Anderson received a call reporting a fallen climber. When Anderson found the patient, Matthew Starkey, he was walking out, holding a shirt on the right side of his head and covered in blood. However, he was conscious and alert. After ensuring the patient's condition was not worsening, Anderson accompanied him on the hike out. Medical assessment revealed a two- to three-inch laceration on the right side of his skull and light rope burns on his leg.

Starkey explained to rescuers that he had been lead climbing outdoors for his first time on the route Chicken Bone (5.8 sport). As he was nearing the third bolt, he lost his grip on a hold and fell. His rope was behind his leg, and this caused him to flip upside down and hit his head on a ledge below. Starkey said he was unsure, but felt like he had "blacked out." He was not wearing a helmet. (*Source: Incident Report from Pilot Mountain State Park.*)

ANALYSIS
This climb has been the scene of numerous accidents over the past couple of years, mostly involving inexperienced climbers. Avoid getting your feet and legs between the rock and the rope. A fall in this position may result in the leg snagging the rope and flipping the climber upside down. While many sport leaders pass on wearing a helmet, this accident is a good example of its usefulness. Leading easier climbs can increase the risk for injury, as they often tend to be lower angle and/or have ledges that a falling climber could hit. (*Source: The Editors.*)

FATAL FALL | Free Soloing
Linville Gorge Wilderness Area, Shortoff Mountain

On June 30, Austin Howell (31) met climber/photographer Ben Wu at the Shortoff Mountain trailhead. Their plan was for Howell to free solo a few routes on Shortoff and have Wu photograph him. Reaching the climbing area, Ben photographed Austin on Tilted World (5.10), Dopey Duck (5.9), and Golden Rule (5.11a/b). After finishing, Wu left and Howell decided to free solo another route.

Two climbers, Riley Collins and Jay Massey, were preparing to climb Dopey Duck when they witnessed Howell fall at around 11:30 a.m. Neither can say for sure what route he was on, but most likely it was in the Tilted World, an area of very steep 5.10 and 5.11 pitches, since his pack was found a couple of days later on top of that zone. Collins stated that, moments before falling, Howell yelled "NO!"

After witnessing the fall, Massey reached the fallen climber and began CPR. At 1:18 p.m., rescue crews arrived at the top of Shortoff Mountain, and a first responder reached Howell soon afterward. He could not be revived.

ANALYSIS

Howell was known to record himself climbing, and on this day his camera filmed the entire incident. Investigators were able to view the video and observed that he had both hands on the rock when his foot slipped. He tried unsuccessfully to regain his footing on the overhanging climb and fell. Free soloing is inherently dangerous, with no room for error, even for the most talented and experienced soloists.

Massey should be praised for his response. He arrived at Howell's side within minutes of the fall, stabilized his position so he didn't slip further down the slope, and initiated CPR until he was asked to leave the scene by dispatch. (*Sources: Facebook post by Susan Hall, personal communications with Corey Winstead and James Robinson (Burke County Rescue Squad), and Ben Wu.*)

FALL ON ROCK | Inexperience, Inadequate Preparation
Linville Gorge Wilderness Area, The Amphitheater

On October 5, an organized college group divided into two parties to expedite climbing the Daddy (500 feet, 5.6). The first group (A) summited and then hiked out to the parking area. Prior to starting, the groups had agreed that if the second group (B) didn't make it to the parking area by 10 p.m., the first group would go back and look for them.

At approximately 6 p.m., while following the last pitch, a male climber (25) fell about 15 feet onto a pyramid-shaped rock, landing on the back of his right knee and lower thigh. He was the last climber in a group of eight students and instructors who had previously topped out. Around 10 p.m., Group A returned to look for the second group, and while en route they received a text from Group B reporting that there had been an incident with injuries. About the same time, a call was made to Burke County SAR indicating that an injured climber was stranded near the top of the Daddy. The overall group leader (who was with Group A) descended to check on the injured climber, before reascending and making contact with search and rescue.

A Burke County SAR member and Burke County EMS Special Ops medic arrived at the informal trail above the Amphitheater and made voice contact with the patient, who was about 90 feet below the top. The rescuers immediately requested further high-angle rescue resources. The weather was wet, foggy, and chilly, with a breeze of about 10 mph. SAR member James Robinson rappelled to the patient and found him partially covered with a plastic poncho and cold and wet. Robinson assisted the climber out of his wet layers and into a warming bag with heat packs. A tarp was used for shelter.

The climber had sustained a muscular injury to the upper right leg that prevented him from bearing weight. Both rescuer and patient were anchored to the wall and spent the remainder of the night on the ledge while resources were assembled. The patient's leg was splinted.

In the early morning, rescuers performed a 3:1 hoist, with Robinson ascending a fixed line alongside the patient to keep him from impacting the rock face. The injured climber was assisted to the parking area and evacuated to a local hospital.

ANALYSIS

The final pitch of the Daddy requires intentional gear placements and an attentive belay to protect the second. A combination of factors contributed to this climber's relatively long fall and injury: 1) an inexperienced belayer, 2) slack in the rope, 3) the climber's weight (approximately 250 pounds) and a narrow rope (8–9mm), both of which would have increased rope stretch, and 4) haste due to approaching darkness.

Climbers venturing into Linville Gorge Wilderness should carry enough equipment to spend the night. This group did not have the necessary gear or clothing for night-time exposure, nor enough food or water, and this affected their decision-making. (*Sources: James Robinson, Corey Winstead, and Adrian Hurst, Burke County SAR.*)

OREGON

FALL ON ICE | Inexperience, Climbing Alone
Mt. Hood, South Side

On May 5, an inexperienced 39-year-old solo climber slipped while traversing a summit route, falling several hundred feet into a fumarole in the Hot Rocks area. With the assistance of another climber who witnessed the fall, he extracted himself, but he had suffered minor abrasions, lacerations, and bruises during the slide. A nearby Portland Mountain Rescue (PMR) member escorted the climber down to the Timberline Ski Area for a medical evaluation. The climber was wearing a helmet, which likely prevented more serious injuries.

ANALYSIS
Solo climbing on Mt. Hood should be undertaken only by experienced climbers. Identifying hazardous conditions, terrain, and changing weather requires experience that is best gained with qualified partners. In some cases, the terrain characteristics (slope, ice, etc.) may make self-arrest exceedingly difficult, even when it's practiced regularly. For difficult surface conditions and high-consequence exposure, climbers should consider using a rope and belay to limit fall distances. When climbing above fumaroles, the risk of toxic gas exposure adds to the danger of falls. (*Source: Jeff Scheetz and Pearce Beissinger, Portland Mountain Rescue.*)

FALL ON ICE | Inexperience
Mt. Hood, South Side

While descending from the summit on December 30, a 16-year-old unroped climber slipped at the Pearly Gates and fell approximately 500 feet into the Devil's Kitchen area. The slide resulted in a femur fracture and a cracked helmet. The injured climber was assisted by his party (seven members) and nearby climbers, including a wilderness first responder. Members of Portland Mountain Rescue and the Hood River Crag Rats assisted with a ground evacuation.

ANALYSIS
Every year climbers are seriously injured due to falls on the South Side of Mt. Hood. Inexperienced climbers should practice snow travel skills, the use of crampons, and

effective self-arrest prior to attempting a climb of the mountain. In climbing parties with varying levels of experience, consider having the strongest member of the team belay the less experienced during key sections of the downclimb. (*Jeff Scheetz and Pearce Beissinger, Portland Mountain Rescue.*)

SMITH ROCK SUMMARY
Smith Rock State Park

On August 24, at approximately 9:40 a.m., Chaitanya Sathe (35), a well-known and admired member of the Mazamas, suffered a fatal fall of approximately 100 feet while descending 3rd- or 4th-class terrain into the Lower Gorge. A number of accidents have occurred over the years on this climber trail, with at least one other fatality (ANAC 2008). Fourth-class climbing or descents require balance and care, particularly when carrying a heavy pack.

Since this accident, several volunteers have worked to make the routes into the Lower Gorge safer for climbers. The Chimney approach has new stainless-steel rungs at the top and a metal ladder at the bottom to replace an old wooden one. There also have been improvements to the steep descent trail (where the above accident occurred), including better steps and flatter surfaces, but climbers nevertheless must remain vigilant while descending.

There were four other reported climbing accidents at Smith Rock. The first was on April 21 on Lion's Jaw (5.8 trad) at the Morning Glory Wall. A belayer was injured when her climbing partner fell and pulled out several pieces of gear; the large fall pulled the belayer into the air, where she collided with the leader. She was able to self-evacuate.

THE CLIMBING GRIEF FUND

Serious accidents always leave more people in need of attention than just the patients themselves. Climbing partners and other survivors may continue to suffer long after a rescue has ended. The American Alpine Club now offers resources to survivors through the Climbing Grief Fund (CGF).

The CGF is expanding the conversation around grief and trauma in the climbing and ski mountaineering communities. It acts as a resource hub to better equip the mental health of our climbing community. Resources include:

- *Individual financial grants* for support related to grief and trauma
- *Story archive:* video, audio, and written story sharing
- *Mental health directory and resources*
- *Psychological education and workshops* (for individuals, organizations, companies)
- *CGF Talks:* online conversations with Sky Yardeni, CGF therapeutic director, and a professional in the field discussing intersections of grief and resilience.

Learn more at americanalpineclub.org/grieffund.

The next day, on Wherever I May Roam (5.9), a popular multi-pitch sport climb, a climber (female, mid-20s) led the first pitch and then incorrectly rigged her belay device (attempting to belay directly from the anchor in "guide mode"). When her partner (male, 20s) fell a couple of bolts up, she was unable to arrest the fall. The climber suffered back and leg injuries, and the belayer suffered rope burns to her hands.

A very similar accident occurred on June 1 at the Red Wall on the first pitch of Super Slab (5.6 trad). Again, after ascending the first pitch, the belayer rigged his device incorrectly in guide mode, and when the second slipped a third of the way up, he was unable to arrest her fall. She suffered back injuries, and the belayer had rope burns on his hands. In both of these incidents, the belayers failed to load their devices correctly for belaying off the bolted anchor. It is essential to get proper instruction and always test that your belay device will lock under a load prior to bringing up the second.

The final reported accident occurred on August 16, when a male climber fell at the pin-scar crux halfway up Sunshine Dihedral (5.12a), pulling out multiple pieces of gear he had placed above the route's first bolt. He fractured his right tibia/fibula.

Evacuations in these incidents were performed by Deschutes County SAR and Redmond Fire Department. (*Source: Deschutes County SAR.*)

TENNESSEE

FALL FROM ANCHOR | Incorrectly Tied Knot
The Obed, Lilly Bluff

On October 3, Rachel Zoeller (35) and her climbing partner were at Lilly Bluff in the Obed. Rachel had been climbing intermittently since 2007, but it had been over a year since she climbed outside, so she and her partner reviewed the process for cleaning a bolted anchor at the practice anchors located at the base of the cliff.

After climbing the sport route Rocking Chair (5.9) on top-rope, Rachel cleaned the anchor, audibly going through the steps with her climbing partner below. After threading the rope through the anchors, Rachel tied an overhand on a bight and attached this to her harness with two opposing draws. Before detaching from the anchor, Rachel had her belayer take out the slack, and she test-weighted the system. After it held, she detached from the anchors and indicated to her belayer that she was ready to lower. She remembers the knot unraveling, and she fell about 60 feet to the ground.

Rachel was not wearing a helmet, but she did not hit her head in the fall and remained conscious during the entire incident. She was airlifted to the University of Tennessee hospital in Knoxville, where she spent ten days in the ICU and was treated for injuries including a partially severed spinal cord, shattered pelvis, internal bleeding, and broken back, ankles, multiple ribs, and sternum. (*Sources: Rachel Zoeller and the National Park Service.*)

ANALYSIS
Rachel's rope was found by responders to have a single overhand knot remaining at the end of the rope. It is possible that Rachel missed the tail end of the rope when

she wrapped a bight around the rope to tie an overhand on a bight (see photos). The resulting partially tied knot can bunch up, appearing as though it were tied correctly and even hold some weight as it tightens. However, with enough weight, the knot turns into a simple slip knot. The tail will pull through the slip knot until it releases, leaving no bight and just an overhand remaining on the rope.

Rachel did a lot of things right. She practiced on the ground and then went through each step with her belayer as she was cleaning the anchor. A tactile check in which the knot was tugged and turned over might have helped her identify that her knot wasn't tied correctly. Testing the knot with a bounce and watching it tighten before untethering can further demonstrate a knot is correct. (Sources: Rachel Zoeller, the National Park Service, and the Editors.)

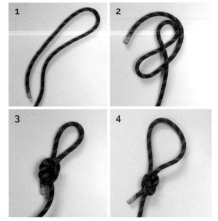

Improperly tied overhand on a bight. (1) Starting loop. (2) Bight wrapped around the rope to start an overhand, but failing to capture the tail. (3) The incomplete knot may have hidden the tail (particularly if the tail was short) and temporarily held weight. (4) Ultimately, the tail would have pulled through, leaving only a single overhand on the rope.

TEXAS

LEADER GROUND FALL | Unable to Clip, Inexperience
Reimer's Ranch, Hand Beyond Wall

On May 26, I was climbing with a less experienced partner at Reimer's Ranch, an area unfamiliar to both of us. After comfortably completing a 5.10 route, I gave my partner (male, 33) the option of leading or top-roping the adjacent route Monkey Boy (5.10c). He decided to lead the route and clipped the first bolt easily. He continued up, and at about 20 feet, he grabbed a jug above his head with the second bolt right next to it. He pulled out slack, attempted to make the clip, then dropped the rope to readjust his hands. This happened several times before he suddenly fell to the ground, injuring his back and knocking out a tooth. Afterward, he said he felt secure but his hands were sweaty and slipped off due to the heat, humidity, and texture of the limestone.

ANALYSIS
The climber had only been lead climbing outdoors once before. As such, I think we should have stuck with climbs that were familiar or easier, so he could gain experience on comfortable climbs. As the belayer, I struggled with whether to give or take in slack when the climber was attempting to make the clip; I believe if I had taken in more of the slack, I may have been able to catch his fall before he hit the ground. I didn't do this because I did not want him to struggle with the rope while clipping. I

also think better communication between the climber and belayer could have helped. [*Editor's Note: This is a very short wall, and it would be difficult for a belayer to keep the climber from hitting the ground in a fall at the second bolt as it's described.*]

The area between the first and second clip is often the most dangerous zone on a sport climb, as a ground fall is possible. There are several options to help mitigate this risk. Stick-clipping the second bolt (if possible) can lessen the chance of a ground fall. In heavily concentrated route areas, bolts may be accessed while lowering from an adjacent route, so the draws can be preplaced and the rope preclipped through the first and possibly the second bolt. (*Sources: The belayer and the Editors.*)

RAPPEL ERROR | Uneven Ropes, Stopper Knot Untied
Enchanted Rock State Park

On October 12, I (age 25) was in a team of five guides setting top-rope anchors for a base-managed site. Three guides left to hike in with our clients while another guide and I finished setting anchors and dropping ropes. We then needed to rappel to the bottom to meet our team. We threaded our last rope and tossed it down but could not see the ends on the ground, and there was no middle marker on the rope. I tethered myself to our anchor and began to set up my rappel, extending my rappel device on nylon webbing and using an autoblock backup. I transitioned to the rappel and began to descend.

At about 15 feet above the ground, I realized that I had reached the end of one strand of my rappel rope. The barrel knot we had tied as a stopper in this strand had run into my autoblock. I tried to pull myself up off the knot so I could fix the issue. In the process, the knot rolled over itself and became undone. The rope ran through my device, and I fell to the ground and rolled down some rocks. Upon landing, I bit my tongue, suffered multiple abrasions on my legs, and had pain at the top of the left side of my pelvis, but we decided I was well enough to stay and complete my day. (*Source: Tuesday Kahl.*)

ANALYSIS

This site was the third choice for the guided group, and they were in a rush to set up top-ropes for their clients. The climbers executed some of the safety steps for a rappel, including closing the system with stopper knots and using an autoblock as a backup. The main item they missed was ensuring both rope ends were on the ground. It is possible the rope they were using was shorter than expected, but this alone would not account for the uneven ends. To prevent this, the climbers could have fed both ends of the rope through the anchor simultaneously until all the rope was out, so they would know the ends were even, despite the lack of a middle mark.

The barrel knot should have prevented the climber from rappelling off the end of the rope. (It is unusual for this knot to "roll" in the manner described.) It's possible this stopper knot was not tied snugly enough and/or there was too little tail, leaving little margin for error as the rappeller worked to separate the knot from her autoblock. "Fingers to elbow" is a good way to measure a generous tail of rope below a stopper knot. In addition, it is crucial to dress knots snugly. (*Sources: Tuesday Kahl and the Editors.*)

UTAH

LOWERING ERROR | Off-Route, Rope Too Short, No Stopper
Ogden, The School Room, Sunday Wall Crag

A group of three moderately experienced climbers—two males and one female (Sam, 23; Jared, 18; and Rylee, 27)—headed to the School Room early on August 15. Rylee and Sam had just finished their Single Pitch Instructor (SPI) courses a day earlier. The climbers flaked the rope below Super Bowl Sunday (5.5 trad, single pitch), racked up, and casually did their safety checks and communication.

Sam led the route easily, placing protection along the way. The beta they'd seen called for using bolted anchors at the top of a nearby route to descend. But when Sam finished the fifth-class terrain, he could not find the bolts. He scrambled a bit higher to look for the anchor, then continued up more fifth-class to the top of the crag. He decided to set up a top-rope from there and wrapped a massive boulder with a double cordelette for an anchor, then called to be lowered. At one point he saw the middle mark of the rope passing and called to his belayer, Jared,

At the top of Super Bowl Sunday, climbers scramble to the right to reach a shared bolted anchor. *Derek DeBruin*

to ask how much rope was left. Jared responded that there should be enough for a top-rope. Sam continued to lower and then began free-falling to the ground.

Sam's right leg took most of the impact. He rolled back and hit his right elbow. The climbers assessed the damage and built a splint for Sam's leg with the equipment they had available. Leaving the rest of their gear to retrieve later, they made the one-mile descent to their vehicles, with Jared assisting Sam and then carrying him with the help of a runner they met on the trail. At an urgent care center, Sam was diagnosed with a fractured talus from his fall of approximately 15 feet.

ANALYSIS

There was no stopper knot in the rope, and none of the climbers checked for one before Sam started climbing. A stopper knot (or tying in the belayer) would have kept Sam from hitting the ground. They were unfamiliar with the cliff and had not researched the descent adequately or spotted the rappel anchor from the ground before climbing. The distance to Sam's top anchor (more than 110 feet) hindered communication. None of the climbers was wearing a helmet, and they were lucky the injuries were not more serious. (*Sources: Sam, Jared, and the Editors.*)

SLIDE ON SNOW | Inadequate Equipment
Wasatch Range, Mt. Olympus, West Slabs

On June 9, Salt Lake County Search and Rescue (SLCOSAR) assisted an injured climber who had fallen while descending Mt. Olympus. A team of three climbers, including

the 27-year-old female, had descended from the West Slabs route, a long, moderate rock climb, and entered the gully at the bottom of the slabs. This approach gully is steep and narrow and often stays filled with snow until early summer. The woman slipped on the snow, and without an ice axe to self-arrest, she slid into a large snow moat. She dropped about 12 to 15 feet into the moat, hitting rocks at the bottom and suffering a puncture wound to her left calf, broken ribs on the right, and an open fracture of her right lower leg.

SLCOSAR sent several members to hike up from the bottom of the mountain, and two members were inserted by helicopter just above the injured party. The two teams got to the patient about the same time and began treating her and prepping her for extraction. The team was able to build snow anchors and move her out of the moat to a location where she could be helicoptered off the mountain.

Rescuers work in a deep moat beside the snow-filled gully below the West Slabs route. *SLCOSAR Photo*

ANALYSIS

There are several descents from this popular route, none of them quick or easy. For the gully approach or descent, an ice axe (and possibly crampons) is recommended for each climber when snow is present. If this climber had been carrying an axe and had the know-how, she likely could have arrested before sliding into the moat. (*Sources: Salt Lake County Search and Rescue and the Editors.*)

LOST ON DESCENT FROM WEST SLABS ROUTE: *On July 28, three female climbers became stranded high on Mt. Olympus after climbing the West Slabs route and getting lost on the descent. The three summited the mountain after completing the climb late in the day and did not locate the descent trail, but instead dropped into Tolcat Canyon to the south of the main trail. Around 10:30 p.m., they called for help. Salt Lake County Search and Rescue members started up the mountain around 12:30 a.m. At 2:30 a.m., a Utah Department of Public Safety helicopter was able to locate and pick up the stranded climbers.*

LEDGE FALL ON ROCK | Inadequate Protection
Wasatch Range, Little Cottonwood Canyon, Pentapitch Area

Two 26-year-old males were involved in a rock climbing accident on the morning of July 12, while attempting a variation to the right of the second lead on Pentapitch. According to the belayer (climber A), he had led the first pitch of Pentapitch and then brought up his partner (climber B), who was planning on leading Sasquatch, the 5.9+ trad variation to the second pitch. It was B's first time climbing in Little Cottonwood Canyon, but he had said he was comfortable climbing on granite.

Climber B placed his first piece, a number 4 Camalot, about five feet up the route, and took a small fall about a foot above that piece. He took a short rest, continued climbing, and, in the thin section of the climb, placed a DMM number 7 offset nut about eight feet above his last piece. B continued up and was trying to place a third piece of gear, another eight or so feet above the DMM nut, when he fell. The offset nut blew out, and although A pulled in some rope as B was falling, the leader dropped an estimated 40 feet and hit a ledge about five feet below the belay station.

Climber B had a severely dislocated ankle and some back injuries. Climber A tied off the fallen climber and gave himself a long leash from the anchor to move down to B. Climber B was conscious and alert, and he called 911 for help at about 10:45 a.m. Climber A tied a tourniquet around B's ankle and got on the phone with paramedics to guide them to the scene. With B's permission, he lowered climber B to the ground and then rappelled to join him. Two other climbers joined them, one of whom was an emergency department doctor, who treated B's injuries while A went to the road to direct responders. At around noon, Climber B was short-hauled from the scene by helicopter, then transported to the hospital, where surgeons repaired the damage.

ANALYSIS
According to climber A, the medium size offset nut that pulled out was not set deeply enough. Only about 3–4 mm of surface area at the edge of the nut showed damage from the fall (less than half the width of this nut). The climb may have been beyond the leading ability of the climber, as he had already fallen below the start of the most difficult climbing on the pitch. Protection opportunities are plentiful on this pitch, and more frequent placements could have prevented B from hitting the ledge. (*Sources: Climber A and the Editors.*)

STRANDED | Unable to Find Rappel in Darkness
Wasatch Range, Little Cottonwood Canyon, Gate Buttress Area

Salt Lake County Search and Rescue (SLCOSAR) was called out October 12 around 9:15 p.m. to assist three experienced out-of-town climbers who were unfamiliar with the area (one male and two females). The trio had climbed a long traditional route known as Tingey's Terror (5.7), completing all seven pitches, but when they finished they were unable to find the way to the rappel station. After scrambling around until after dark, and with a cold night setting in, they called for help.

An SLCOSAR team went to the base of the wall and talked with the climbers several times on the phone while guiding them down toward a rappel station, with the help of large lights. The climbers were then able to rappel two pitches to the SAR team's location and walk back to the trailhead. None of the climbers had any injuries.

ANALYSIS
All the climbers had headlamps but were unable to find the descent and wisely called for help rather than risk a fall in exposed terrain. The most frequent rappel descent from Tingey's Terror is at the Schoolroom area, which involves a substantial scramble down to the west and is fairly difficult to locate in daytime, let alone once it is dark. With three climbers planning a long route in an unfamiliar area, they would have been wise to start earlier, leaving ample time to find the descent route before dark. (*Sources: Salt Lake County Search and Rescue and the Editors.*)

AVALANCHES | Poor Position, Failure to Heed Danger Signs
Wasatch Range, Santaquin Canyon

Shane and I (both in our 40s and experienced climbers) arrived at the base of the Squash Head ice route (WI 3/4) around 9:45 a.m. on February 2. We saw two climbers finishing the first pitch. The avalanche forecast for the day reported the hazard as "low" at the climb's elevation and "moderate" at middle and upper elevations. Upon our arrival, it was encouraging to see the route not dripping and other climbers on it. However, the temperatures were already in the mid to upper 30s. Our climbing plan would have us down by noon.

As Shane led the first pitch, other climbers arrived. I followed Shane's lead and was on the low-angle ramp above the first steep section when an avalanche funneled from the gully above the route. The slide passed Shane at the belay, then passed over me as I ducked behind an ice bulge. The four or five climbers at the base jumped away as one or two feet of snow piled up. After some "all safe" communication, I quickly finished the ramp to the anchor. The parties above us had evidently reached the top of the second pitch and exited via an alternate rappel toward the route Backoff. The parties at the base were mostly packing up to leave.

That first slide was at 11 a.m. I met Shane in the belay alcove on climber's left, both of us full of adrenaline. Our discussion is hard to recall, but ultimately we made a nearly fatal decision to continue up the second pitch. In retrospect, that was the moment we lost control of the day's outcome. There were four more avalanches to come.

Shane and I had climbed this route together seven years prior, and Shane had climbed it since. Before our earlier ascent, we had studied Google Earth and concluded the route was mostly protected from avalanche terrain by a ridge that runs diagonally above. In fact, the route is a funnel from avalanche slopes far up the mountain. During our short discussion at the belay, Shane and I concluded the slide had probably originated as a wet sluff not far above the route. We figured the sluff had unloaded the gully and that another slide was unlikely. In our decision process, we ignored the real possibility that the avalanche had originated as a wet slide much higher up.

I led the second pitch. Near the top of the steeper ice, another small sluff passed. I was within view of the anchor and decided to place my final screw and scramble up the gully for 50 feet to the two-bolt anchor. There, I clipped in with my tether and set up Shane's belay on an ATC Guide in autoblock mode. Shane was trailing the second rope we needed to rappel. With Shane ready to climb, I gave three tugs to signal "on belay." At that moment, I felt a much stronger rumble than the previous slides. I looked up the gully and saw a very large avalanche turn into the gully 200 feet directly above me. There was nowhere to hide. I thought I was dead.

My belay was in the slide path, but to reach the anchor bolts the gully would need to fill 10 to 12 feet deep with snow before. After two screams of "avalanche," fast-moving snow was upon me. Almost gently, I was lifted onto the surface of a river of snow. The gully finally stopped filling just one foot below the bolts. My body was horizontal, head uphill, held by my PAS tether. I rode on top of the snow river for about a minute, and then, as the snow receded, it set me down in the same stance I had occupied a minute earlier. The toe of this slide reached the logging road below the route.

Rattled but unhurt, I tugged on the rope to check on Shane. (We could not communicate verbally due to the terrain and distance.) I felt three tugs back, but it was quickly evident we could not communicate an evacuation plan through rope tugs. Shane had weathered the slide in the first belay alcove, getting lightly pummeled by snow.

Shane climbed the second pitch quickly. He left most of the screws on the route and then clipped into the anchor chain. Over the next ten minutes, we were hit by a fourth and a fifth slide as we planned our escape and prepared the rappel. These were smaller but still jostled us both strongly. The fourth slide ripped Shane's trailing rope and ATC from gear loops on his harness.

We briefly considered finding a safe location and waiting for colder temps to stabilize the snow but worried about remaining exposed in this position. We also considered the nearby Backoff rappel and ruled it out because we mistakenly believed that rap required two ropes.

We decided to tie our 70-meter lead rope to our anchor and rappel down a single strand. Lacking a belay device, Shane rapped on a Munter. Soon we were both in the first-pitch alcove and relatively safe from danger. We were able to cut off a 50-foot tail of the lead rope,

Avalanche debris below the Squash Head ice route in Santaquin Canyon following the slides reported here. *Brian Crozier*

downclimb the low-angle ramp at the top of the first pitch (somewhat out of the slide path), and use a V-thread anchor to descend the final 30-foot curtain to the ground.

ANALYSIS

Our failures this day were related to poor knowledge of the route's avalanche danger and descent options, complacency due to a "low" avy forecast, and improper decision-making after the danger became evident. We let the excitement of climbing together after years and the good weather cloud our judgment. Lessons learned:

(1) Avalanche danger above ice climbs is often not visible.

(2) We failed to recognize the initial small wet slides as a precursor to larger, solar-triggered avalanches higher up the mountain.

(3) More conservative decision-making was needed after observations of local conditions contradicted the day's avalanche rating.

(4) We should have refreshed our route knowledge. Significant avalanche reports from Squash Head are available online that were not present when we first researched the route years earlier.

(5) We didn't adequately research descent options. We had a poor understanding of the alternate rappel that could have reduced our time in the avalanche zone.

(6) Personal radios could have reduced our exposure time by facilitating escape planning after the largest slide hit us, while we were still separated at two belays. (*Source: Brian Crozier.*)

EDITOR'S NOTE: *Warmer winters and more frequent rain events may be increasing the avalanche hazard on many Utah ice climbs. About a year after this incident, in early March 2020, the Utah Avalanche Center reported another large wet-snow avalanche (containing significant log debris) on the Squash Head climb.*

LEADER FALL | Off-Route, Loose Hold
Southeast Utah, Castle Valley, Sister Superior

On November 14, my brother David (32) and I (29) set out to climb Jah Man (5 pitches, 5.10c) on Sister Superior. In the days leading up to the climb, we had read route descriptions and the most recent trip reports. As we racked up, I picked out features on the first pitch that appeared to match the route description. Specifically, I identified what I understood to be the "squeeze chimney" up and right of the start.

Leading the first pitch, I got to the early ledge and then wrestled through a V-slot/squeeze that felt scrappier than the 5.8/5.9 described. At the top of this squeeze, I found two large fixed nuts with a sling. I clipped my own sling to them and continued up. At this point, I could tell I was beginning to trend left of where I should be, but the slot and gear that I had passed led me to believe I was still on route.

Above the two nuts, the climbing eased into low fifth class, and I carefully explored a series of ledges for the correct route. As confusion overcame confidence, I decided to stop and build an anchor so David and I could regroup. The first two crack systems I evaluated appeared to have some unstable rock. As I continued searching, I placed both hands on the face in front of me and leaned back. A block peeled off in my hands and I tumbled backward, falling 25 feet before the fixed nuts and rope caught me.

Immediately upon stopping, I saw blood dripping briskly from my pant leg. David lowered me to the ground. My left elbow was in excruciating pain. Quickly realizing I would be unable to walk back to the trailhead, David called 911 and guided responders to our location. A helicopter arrived, but because I was located in a narrow band of relatively level ground between a sandstone tower and a steep scree slope, the extraction was complicated. Eventually I was evacuated to Grand Junction, where I was treated for a major laceration on my lower leg and a shattered left elbow.

ANALYSIS

During the week preceding the trip, I had been working long hours, totaling 80 hours in six days. The morning I finished my last night shift, I immediately jumped on a plane from Seattle to Denver without sleeping. The next day we drove to Utah, and we headed up to Sister Superior the following morning. In retrospect, sleep deprivation and work-related stress likely contributed to my poor route-finding.

There were many clues that I was off route, but I misinterpreted these as signs that I was following the route description. Specifically, I should have recognized the two nuts as bail gear from someone who had also followed the wrong slot. I also should have corroborated written descriptions with closer attention to photos of the route. Finally, I had noted instability in the rock, but was falsely confident because of the very easy climbing in the area where I fell. Given this low-angle terrain, I should have been more cognizant of the risk inherent in a fall. (*Source: Whitney Kiker.*)

SECOND JAH MAN ACCIDENT: *One day after the incident described here, a 20-year-old woman took a ground fall from the first pitch of Jah Man when her sole piece of protection pulled out. She was flown from the scene by helicopter. Search "Jah Man ground fall" at publications.americanalpineclub.org for the full report. In early January 2020, less than two months after these incidents, the start of this classic climb and the huge flake forming the squeeze chimney collapsed. The original route is no longer climbable.*

VIRGINIA

GROUND FALL | Failed to Clip Second Bolt
Hidden Valley

On April 6, a climber (age 22) was leading the sport route Axis Bold as Butta (5.11a) at Hidden Valley, a crag near Abingdon. She had led the route several times previously. The first bolt, 11 feet off the ground, was stick-clipped. There is a good stance about a foot above the first bolt, and taller climbers are able to make the next clip from here. Because of her height, the climber was unable to reach the second bolt from this stance, and as she moved up, her foot slipped. Although her fall was slowed by her belayer, she landed on the ground after swinging under an overhang at the start of the climb. She sustained a fractured left calcaneus and a fractured nose.

ANALYSIS
The area around the second bolt is often the most vulnerable zone of a sport climb because a slip before making the second clip can result in a ground fall. Stick-clipping the second bolt is sometimes an option. In areas with heavily concentrated routes, bolts on one climb may be accessed from adjacent routes. (In this case, lowering from the 5.8+ route beside Axis would have allowed the climbers to hang a quickdraw and/or clip the rope at the second bolt before attempting the lead.) A third option is the "stiffy" quickdraw, which has a long, rigid dogbone for out-of-reach bolts. This is available commercially as the Kong Panic, or it can be fashioned at home; an article in *Climbing* magazine (available online) describes one method for this. (*Source: Jeff Sanders.*)

WASHINGTON

FALL ON ICE, CREVASSE FALL | Roped With No Protection
Mt. Baker, Squak Glacier

About 6:30 a.m. on August 31, a male climber (54) was injured while trying to ascend Mt. Baker via the Squak Glacier. His party of three roped climbers was moving up the dry, bare-ice glacier using a 60-meter rope, with approximately 10 meters between each climber. The middle climber slipped after turning a corner and fell, pulling the lead climber and the trailing climber off their feet. The leader was pulled into a four-foot-deep crevasse, where he became wedged, thus arresting his fall as well as the slides of his partners. The leader suffered numerous injuries, including a puncture wound and fractured lower jaw from his ice axe, three fractured ribs, and a fractured wrist. The middle and trailing climbers suffered only minor bruising.

ANALYSIS
The Squak Glacier is considered an easy snow climb in spring and early summer, and while climbers will be roped up for crevasses, running protection (screws, pickets,

etc.) is typically not used. In late season, glaciers in the Cascades often have a firm snow or hard ice surface, and stopping a slip from becoming a slide is difficult. Protection should be considered. The distance between climbers on the rope drastically affects the ability to hold a fall. Typically, climbers should stay closer together on bare ice or firm conditions. On easy ground, consider unroping to not jeopardize the entire team. (*Sources: Kaf Adventures and the Editors.*)

RAPPEL ANCHOR FAILURE | Loose Rock, Overconfidence
North Cascades, Eldorado Peak, West Ridge

Sam Weichert (30), Matt Skorina (26), and I (24) were planning to climb the West Ridge of Eldorado Peak (alpine terrain plus 10 pitches up to 5.8) and the Southwest Buttress on Dorado Needle (13 pitches, 5.7) over five days in August to help Skorina prepare for his AMGA advanced alpine course. Weichert and I are also aspiring alpine guides, one to two years behind Skorina in the progression. The approach to these climbs took longer than expected (1.5 days), and we were all tired from a summer of alpine work. Skorina had a bad cold.

On August 14, Skorina was mock guiding us on the West Ridge route, and Weichert and I were both end-roped on our single-rated 8.9mm rope. Progress was slow, and as we approached the crux at 4 p.m., still 1,700 feet below the top, our planned summit bivy seemed unlikely. Looking at a hard-to-protect 5.8 slab traverse under a chossy downclimb, we decided to bail back down the ascent route after seven pitches.

We were set up at an obvious notch before the first tower on the ridge, and our first rappel anchor was set back behind a block. The rope ran around a sharp corner, and we spent several minutes padding it. We rigged for a 60-meter single-line rappel, planning for a rappeller to place protection so Skorina could then down-lead the pitches and avoid leaving gear for intermediate anchors.

I rapped first since I was the heaviest. As soon as I loaded the rope, the rope slipped off the padding. I was leaning back and about to drop over a lip (five feet from the stance) when I saw the sheath shredding and the core exposed. I was barely able to unweight the rope before the core cut. Had I fallen, it would have been a deadly fall. We isolated the core shot in a butterfly knot and re-rigged for double-strand 30-meter rappels. These went well, and we were able to conserve gear. (We had 12 cams and many rappels remaining.) As we descended, the rock quality deteriorated and we had to look harder for anchors.

One to two raps before a 3rd-class ramp led to a flat spot on the ridge where we expected to bivy, Weichert built a temporary anchor at a hanging stance, using a crack that appeared to be between two structural pieces of rock, with a number 1 and number 0.75 cam. A hard thwack on the more suspect side of the crack (a vertical column) suggested it was solid, and I inspected the gear before clipping in. We both fully weighted the anchor for several minutes while Skorina rappelled to us.

As Weichert and I waited, we decided we could sling the column forming one side of the crack (about one square foot on top and 10 feet tall) and use this for a rappel anchor if we could clean some debris from the back of the crack. Skorina arrived and began cleaning the slot as Weichert and I waited, clipped to personal tethers. As Skorina cleaned, the column shifted and both cams in the crack released. Weichert and I both fell approximately 15 feet into a small gully before tumbling down loose, steep 3rd-class terrain for another 50 feet. We slowed and stopped as the ridge flattened and widened.

Skorina was able to downclimb to reach us. Both Weichert and I were injured, but it was immediately clear that her injuries were more serious than mine. We immediately pressed the SOS button on our Garmin inReach and were in contact with the National Park Service in 20 minutes. By this time, it was about 6:45 p.m. and the sun was setting, so we prepared for an evening on the ridge; neither Weichert nor I could move over technical terrain with our injuries. However, a Navy helicopter was able to rescue us via long line at approximately 9 p.m. (in the dark and with night-vision goggles!) and fly us to Seattle. I had a broken left wrist and torn right bicep, and Weichert ended up with a concussion and the worst bruises of her life.

ANALYSIS
The obvious analysis is that a two-piece, one-feature anchor was insufficient. But in that situation, we were either going to downclimb steep, chossy 4th-class terrain or rappel. The rock looked solid—or at least as solid as anything we'd used already (a heuristic trap).

The more subtle but important takeaway was our mindset. All three of us are working alpine guides, hot off big seasons crushing easy objectives and looking like heroes in front of clients. That obviously will generate some hubris. Add to the mix the fact that Weichert and I were more relaxed on beta and planning than usual because Skorina was "guiding" us, yet our expectations for planning and risk assessment differed from his, and we should have discussed this as a group.

We all had our minds elsewhere as well. I had a high-stakes trip coming up, Skorina had his advanced alpine course, and Weichert was joining a new company. None of us totally had our head in the game. The final, and perhaps most interesting, issue was that the AMGA had used this route for an advanced alpine course two weeks before we got there. Every time the rock quality deteriorated or the climbing got worse, we looked at each other and shrugged, saying, "The AMGA uses this route." This "AMGA stamp of approval" created a bizarre expert halo. [Editor's Note: It's not unusual for guides to belay two clients on a single rope, and these climbers were in the middle of an extended traverse and thus trying to save weight. However, doing alpine routes with two ropes will greatly speed an unplanned retreat and provide access to many more anchor options.] (Source: Spencer Dillon.)

LOWERING ERROR | No Stopper Knot
Index, Lookout Point, Rattletale Wall

Cherry Mayangitan (38) and I (39) were climbing Chasin' the Lizard (5.10a trad) at the Rattletale Wall. I had just finished leading the route and was being lowered by my partner, who was planning to follow and clean. Approximately 20 feet from the ground, my partner felt the end of the 70-meter rope move through her brake hand and then stop in her Grigri.

The rubberized cap at the end of the rope (which was new at the time) had caught in the Grigri and was the only thing preventing the rope from slipping all the way through the device. I quickly clipped in direct to a cam (my first piece), which fortunately was at my waist. I then asked my partner to carefully scramble up toward me, keeping me on belay, until she could free the rope from the Grigri. I untied and we both downclimbed to the belay spot.

ANALYSIS
Both the guidebook and Mountain Project mention that a 70-meter rope will not get you all the way down to the ground while lowering. We should have read the descriptions more closely, tied a knot at the end of the rope (or tied in the belayer), or used two ropes to descend. (*Sources: Patrick Beeson and the Editors.*)

DEADLY ROCKFALL AT THUMB ROCK
Mt. Rainier, Liberty Ridge

At about 8:30 p.m. on May 29, a climber called 911 to report a large rockfall around 10,800 feet at Thumb Rock, high camp for the Liberty Ridge route. The climber relayed to dispatchers that Arleigh William "Bill" Dean (46) had been killed and two other climbers were seriously injured by the rockfall. Weather and the late hour kept rescuers from conducting a rescue until the next day.

The injured and deceased were members of three separate teams attempting Liberty Ridge. The first team arrived at Thumb Rock around noon. Dean's team followed at about 2 p.m. The last group showed up at 3 p.m. They spaced their three tents three to four feet vertically from each other on a slope, with Dean's tent in the middle. The afternoon was hot, with slushy snow, sliding snow, and multiple rockfall incidents. All six climbers were inside their tents when the rockfall occurred just before sunset.

A climber in the lowest tent said he was listening to music but had left one earbud out to listen for rockfall. He'd even joked about wearing a helmet to bed. As the sun waned, he heard yelling and felt rocks graze his back and neck. Dean's tent was pushed partially on top of the lowest tent. The uninjured climbers exited their tents and began to treat those who were hurt. One climber called 911, and another hit the SOS button on his Garmin device. After learning rescuers would not be coming that night, they wrapped the injured climbers to keep them warm and stayed awake to watch for more rockfall.

The next morning, low clouds complicated the rescue operation. A helicopter airlifted the first injured climber around 12:30 p.m., transporting him to Harborview Medical Center in Seattle. The next climber was lifted from the scene about 2:10 p.m. Just before 3 p.m., Dean's body was flown off the mountain. The uninjured climbers began descending from Thumb Rock around 11:15 a.m. and were evacuated from the Carbon Glacier at about 4:30 that afternoon. (*Source: Mt. Rainier National Park incident report.*)

ANALYSIS
This route is known to be committing, with rockfall and falling ice quite common. (See "Danger Zones: Mt. Rainier" in ANAC 2014.) In May 2014, six climbers were swept to their deaths from the ridge while sleeping, presumably by rockfall or a snow slide. Although it's difficult to protect against rockfall at Thumb Rock, it's sometimes possible to build or enhance protective walls around tents. Weather also

played a role in this accident. The climbers reported slushy conditions and rockfall, and the snow hadn't frozen the night before. The park service recommends against attempting Liberty Ridge if the freezing level on Mt. Rainier is above 14,000 feet. Very strong climbers with good climbing conditions may consider camping at Curtis Ridge and then approaching and climbing Liberty Ridge in a single day (normally two days for most climbers), thus minimizing the exposure to falling rock and ice. (*Source: The Editors.*)

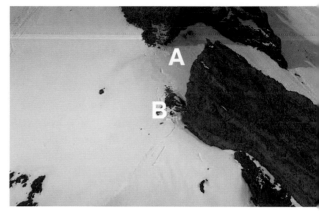

Thumb Rock area showing (A) rockfall impact craters in hard snow and (B) tent site where climbers were hit on the evening of May 29. *NPS Photo*

STRANDED | Weather, Exhaustion
Mt. Rainier, Liberty Ridge

On May 31, a team of four climbers set out from White River Campground to climb Liberty Ridge. Three days later, Yevgeniy Krasnitskiy (39), Ruslan Khasbulatov (33), Vasily Aushev (35), and Constantine Toporov (37) called 911 to report they were stranded at 13,500 feet, still about 600 feet below Liberty Cap, due to high wind and one of the men suffering from altitude sickness and exhaustion. Rangers attempted to reach the men with a park helicopter three times on June 3 and 4. A Chinook helicopter from Joint Base Lewis-McChord near Tacoma also responded, but clouds and wind up to 50 mph stopped all the rescue attempts.

The wind had destroyed the climbers' tent, and they had lost a pack with gear and food. Rescuers attempted to drop supplies, but the men were unable to reach them. By June 5, the weather had worsened on the upper mountain, preventing aerial operations. However, the four men were able to climb about half a mile from their previous location, reaching a point near Liberty Cap that was much less affected by the wind. In a brief window of good weather on the morning of June 6, the park helicopter landed near the stranded climbers and flew them out in two groups. The men were treated briefly at a hospital for exposure and frostbite. (*Sources: Mt. Rainier National Park and news reports.*)

ANALYSIS
Conditions on big mountains change rapidly, and climbers should carry enough clothing, equipment, food, and fuel for unexpected delays. These climbers had heard about a rockfall fatality on Liberty Ridge two days before they started (see report above), so they chose not to camp at the usual Thumb Rock site and instead pushed higher. That last-minute decision contributed to their fatigue and positioned them in a very exposed spot when bad weather moved in. Nonetheless, their ability to reach Liberty Cap on their own greatly facilitated their rescue. (*Sources: News reports and the Editors.*)

WEST VIRGINIA

LOOSE BLOCK, LEDGE FALL | Failure to Test Holds
Seneca Rocks, South Peak, East Face, Lower Skyline Area

Two climbers arrived at the bolted anchors atop the first pitch of Sky Line Traverse on June 2, planning to climb Rear Entry (5.8) to the Lower Broadway ledge. The leader, Mike (50), traversed up and right to a large block that marks the beginning of that climb. As he pulled on the microwave-size block, it came loose, causing him to fall approximately 25 feet and hit a ledge. (The block also fell, almost hitting another party below.) His uninjured partner lowered him to the base of Skyline, atop a ledge about 30 feet above the ground that can be accessed by a short fifth-class scramble.

A nearby climber ran to the local climbing shop, the Gendarme, to activate emergency services. (There is no cell service at Seneca Rocks as it falls within the National Radio Quiet Zone, a designation that prevents interference from cell phones and other electronics for the National Radio Astronomy Observatory.) The injured climber, who was momentarily unconscious after the fall, suffered a large contusion/abrasion below his right ear, along with multiple other abrasions. Guides from Seneca Rocks Climbing School administered first aid and, along with nearby climbers, assisted in the evacuation of the climber to a nearby helipad. The climber was wearing a helmet, which likely prevented far more serious injuries. (*Source: Nick Ingalls.*)

ANALYSIS
Always test blocks and suspect holds by rapping on them and listening and looking for signs they might be loose. Additionally, it's a good idea to gather recent beta about your planned route. A post on the Rear Entry route page at Mountain Project on March 22, about 10 weeks before the accident, indicated this block was loose and ready to fall, and that it was a hazard not only for the climber but also for parties below, and that it could be avoided with care. (*Sources: Nick Ingalls and the Editors.*)

GROUND FALL | Slip on Wet Rock, No Protection
Seneca Rocks, South Peak, West Face

On June 11, Doug (52) and his partner were planning to lead Ecstasy Junior, a popular two-pitch 5.4 on the lower west face of the south peak of Seneca. They opted to begin the climb from above the traditional ramp, eliminating a half pitch of vegetated 5th-class climbing. About 10 feet into his pitch, the leader slipped on wet rock, falling to the ground and fracturing his leg. (*Source: Nick Ingalls.*)

ANALYSIS
The night before there had been significant rain in the area, and the rock was still wet. This was the primary cause of the fall. There are few good gear options here, and the leader had placed no protection before his fall. Waiting for the rock to dry can make the difference between a 5.4 route being an enjoyable cruise or a dangerous undertaking. (*Sources: Nick Ingalls and the Editors.*)

RAPPEL ERRORS | Simul-rappel, Inexperience
Seneca Rocks, South Peak, West Face

At approximately 2 p.m. on July 6, two climbers (males, age 13 and unknown) were attempting to descend from the South Peak via the Pleasant Overhang rappel station on the west face. They had chosen to simul-rappel but did not know they needed two 70-meter ropes to complete the full rappel (or two 60-meter ropes if using an intermediate station).

They unknowingly rappelled past the intermediate station to just above the roof on the second pitch of Pleasant Overhangs (5.7) and did not have the technical ability to ascend their ropes to regain the station. They were able to move to a stance, and another party nearby attempted to assist them by suggesting they climb the second pitch of Pleasant Overhangs and rappel from there. The climbers were unsure about their ability to climb the second pitch, and after seeing a bolt on the nearby Pleasant Exposure (5.7 sport), they decided to continue their descent using it. They then rigged a second rappel from a carabiner on the single bolt.

At approximately 2:15 p.m., they began simul-rappelling again, with the older climber descending much faster than the younger climber before losing control for unknown reasons and rappelling off his end of the rope. Since they were simul-rappelling, his fall unweighted the counter-balance and, according to two eyewitness accounts, the younger climber then fell approximately 100 feet to the ground. The younger climber impacted the top edge of a very steep dirt slope, collapsing the slope and tumbled an additional 30 feet.

Nearby climbers and local guides responded immediately. Guides contacted emergency services and, based on the length of the fall, requested a helicopter for evacuation. The younger climber never lost consciousness after the fall and suffered injuries to his left wrist, left femur, and right foot. Additionally, he had multiple lacerations and abrasions. Rescuers maintained spinal precautions as they placed him in a litter and utilized numerous low-angle rappels to reach Roy Gap Road and a waiting ambulance. The older climber, having fallen only ten feet, had no obvious injuries.

ANALYSIS
This accident was the result of multiple and compounded errors, beginning with a lack of familiarity with the descent options at Seneca. Reading the guidebook and knowing the required rope length and locations of descent anchors would have given the climbers safer options.

Simul-rappelling is an advanced technique and requires careful execution. There are several ways to close the system and prevent a climber who loses control from breaking the essential counter-balance. These include tying knots at the ends of the rope, friction hitch (third hand) backups, and a tether between the climbers, allowing one climber to stop and control the other's descent in the event that one of the climbers loses control of the brake strand.

Finally, tunnel vision while in a stressful situation is extraordinarily difficult to self-identify, and other climbers are often in a position to spot an unseen problem. If, as happened here, another party offers suggestions, take this as an opportunity to stop and reexamine your system and plan. (*Sources: Nick Ingalls and the Editors.*)

OFF ROUTE | Protection Pulled Out
Seneca Rocks, South Peak, West Face

On July 6, a climber was attempting to lead the first pitch of a popular 5.8 trad route called the Burn. According to witnesses, the leader climbed toward the roof but veered significantly right and off route, intersecting the first pitch of Ecstasy (3 pitches, 5.7). The leader then corrected back left to regain the route, resulting in the formation of a large "Z" of rope running through his protection. After pulling through the roof, the leader fell and two pieces came out before a third stopped his descent. The leader suffered a fracture of the tibia and fibula. He refused assistance from other climbers, and he and his partner proceeded to self-rescue. (*Source: Nick Ingalls.*)

ANALYSIS
Staying on route likely would have minimized the seriousness of the fall and resulting injuries to the leader. Creating a "Z" of rope resulted in upward or sideways forces on the placed pieces and likely contributed to a much longer fall. Prior to any climb, study the associated topos and read the available beta to prevent getting off-route. When a climb zigzags, arrange your protection and use extensions to keep the rope running as straight as possible. (*Sources: Nick Ingalls and the Editors.*)

FALL ON ROCK | Ledge Fall, Inexperience
New River Gorge, Bubba City, Beer Wall

In the morning of September 22, my partner (male, 34) and I (female, 38) were climbing at the Beer Wall. We had hoped to warm up on a 5.4, but the route was taken, so we chose Daisy Cutter, a nearby 5.7 sport route. My partner led. The route begins in a chimney before moving out left to the face and a good ledge. He fell twice while attempting to reach the anchors above the ledge. On the first attempt, his thigh hit the ledge, he flipped over, and he fell head first inside of the chimney below the ledge. On his second attempt, he scraped his thigh again on the ledge. He was wearing a helmet that likely saved his forehead from a nasty laceration. He did suffer a lot of bruises, scrapes, and cuts, so we decided to head out and get them all cleaned and bandaged. (*Sources: Matt Smith and Anonymous.*)

ANALYSIS
This route is known to have bad fall potential due to the positioning of the bolted protection, especially between the described ledge and the anchors. In addition, the leader said, "I may have misread the route. I thought a 5.7 would be relatively easy for me. I was about ten months into climbing, and it was my first time at the New River Gorge. I overestimated my skills at a new climbing location." (*Sources: Matt Smith and the Editors.*)

The initial chimney on Daisy Cutter (5.7) at the New River Gorge. *Sebastian Jooster*

WYOMING

RAPPEL ERROR | Uneven Ropes, Haste, No Stopper Knots
Yellowstone National Park, Mammoth Hot Springs, Hoodoos Area

My significant other/climbing partner and I (male, age 20) had spent most of August 6 sightseeing around Yellowstone. After seven hours of driving, I got antsy and checked Mountain Project to see if there were any climbs nearby. I found a 5.5 and 5.9 in the Hoodoos area, near Mammoth Hot Springs, that were easy to top-rope and had a short approach.

My partner and I scrambled up the backside of the crag to check it out. The anchor was odd, with a few chopped bolts, a single homemade bolt ten feet down the face, and a small dying tree. We scrambled down to the car and I racked up. Despite having a helmet, I consciously decided not to grab it because, after looking at the route, I thought, "Ya know, if I fall from the top while setting up this top-rope, a helmet isn't going to help." I climbed back up and constructed a monster anchor consisting of five cams and the trunk of the not-so-great tree. I think the rock is volcanic tuff, and it felt a bit soft, so I wanted as many pieces as I could get, even for a top-rope.

After the anchor was set up, I pulled out our 70-meter rope and dropped it onto the ledge at my feet. Two days prior to this trip, I had been on the Diamond in Colorado, and I was confident that we had center-coiled it before hiking off Longs Peak. It was pretty tangled, but I knew that Mountain Project had listed one of the routes as 25 feet in height, and even though this route obviously was taller than that, I assumed both sides of my rope would reach the ground.

I clipped a bight into the master point and tossed off the rope. I heard it hit and saw portions of it on the ground. The climb is vertical down low, which made it hard to see both strands running all the way to the ground. But I assumed both ends were down, since I believed I had grabbed the rope near the center. The route was so short that I failed to tie safety knots in the ends.

I clipped in my ATC, attached a klemheist backup, and, after weighting my system, unclipped my PAS and started backing off. I rappelled somewhere around 15 feet before stopping to admire an interesting horizontal slot; I thought, "Wow, that's going to be fun to use," and then continued rappelling. Almost immediately, I went weightless and tipped backward, falling about 26 feet. I impacted the ground with the heel of my right foot before landing hard on my right wrist and hand. Blood gushed from my right wrist, and my right shoe was mostly ripped off, but I was alert and awake.

I yelled for my partner, and she ran to get a first-aid kit from the car as I held pressure on my wrist. She then did a quick, focused spine assessment before addressing my other injuries. After trying to close the laceration on my wrist with butterfly bandages, I moved to the car and we drove to the park medical clinic, luckily only ten minutes away. Unluckily, it had closed 45 minutes earlier. The nearest ER was 60 miles to the north in Livingston, Montana. An hour and 20 minutes later, we pulled up to the entrance. My injuries included a sprained ankle, a sprained right wrist, a lacerated right hand, abrasions covering large portions of my back, and contusions on my elbow, head, and right heel.

ANALYSIS

The most obvious way to prevent this accident would have been making sure the rope was placed into the anchor's master point exactly at the middle. I also could have tied knots in the ends of the rope, I could have watched the rope carefully as I backed off the anchor to see if both strands were going all the way to the ground, and I could have asked my partner, who was waiting around the corner in the shade, if both sides were on the ground. I also could have worn a helmet, which would have prevented one of my various injuries. Slowing down and paying more attention to detail would have prevented this accident. (*Source: Anonymous.*)

A typical moat alongside a rock slab in the Tetons. A small opening may lead to a deep cavern that extends far underneath the snowfield, creating a serious falling hazard. *NPS Photo*

FALL INTO MOAT | Hypothermia
Grand Teton National Park, Teewinot

On July 25, a very experienced 71-year-old climber called for help from Teewinot, where he was climbing the standard east face route. At around 10:30 a.m., while attempting to transition onto rock at 10,500 feet from the top of a large snowfield, he broke through the snow surface and fell 20 to 40 feet into a moat. The climber spent the next hour digging himself out of the slot, as meltwater ran down and soaked him. He suffered injuries to his lower extremities, right shoulder (possible dislocation), several abrasions, and hypothermia with severe shivering. He called for help around noon.

A helicopter happened to be in the area, training with rangers, and was able to respond immediately. After flying by to view the accident site with three rangers on board, the helicopter was rigged for short-haul at the Lupine Meadows rescue cache, and two rangers were inserted at about 1 p.m. A medical evaluation determined the need for immediate evacuation via screamer suit due to worsening hypothermia. The patient arrived back in Lupine Meadows at about 1:30 p.m.

After rewarming and evaluation by medical personnel from the park ambulance, the patient declined further medical assistance and self-transported to St. John's Medical Center in Jackson, where he was treated. (*Source: Grand Teton National Park Search and Rescue Report.*)

ANALYSIS

Moats are the crevasse-like slots that form between steep alpine snowfields and adjacent rock walls. They are serious hazards to climbers or skiers falling from above or, as in this case, trying to transition from snow to rock or vice-versa. Because rock walls frequently angle underneath a snowpack, a climber or skier may slide far underneath the snow and be trapped. Rescue can be more difficult than from a similar depth of crevasse. In this case, the climber was alone and thus had little chance of outside help. He was fortunate he was able to escape before dangerously weakening from hypothermia and his injuries. (*Source: The Editors.*)

FALL ON SNOW | Inadequate Equipment, Inexperience
Grand Teton National Park, Middle Teton

At about 5:45 p.m. on July 17, the Jenny Lake rangers were notified of an injured 17-year-old female below the south side of Middle Teton. Rangers were immediately summoned to the Lupine Meadows Rescue Cache, as was the park's contract helicopter. At about 6:40 p.m., helicopter 35HX departed from the rescue cache with rangers P. Edmonds and K. Kreis onboard. They located the party west of the base of the Ellingwood Couloir on the Middle Teton; however, they encountered very strong winds and were unable to land.

Information from other climbers in the area indicated the injured person had fallen and hit some rocks near the saddle between Middle and South Tetons. She felt that she had broken her leg, but there were no life-threatening injuries and no obvious bleeding. Four members of her original group of 11 were with her, and they had helped her descend a short distance to the current location near the base of the Ellingwood. She felt that she could not continue down.

Because of the high winds, a ground operation was initiated. At 7:50 p.m., rangers G.R. Fletcher and V. Zeilman were dispatched from the Lower Saddle, where they were on patrol. They climbed over the Middle Teton and descended to her location via the Southwest Couloir. Rangers R. Schuster and P. Edmonds were dispatched from the rescue cache in the valley.

Both parties of rangers reached the patient at about 11 p.m. Ranger Schuster interviewed her and learned that after a successful ascent of the Middle Teton by the Southwest Couloir route, she had slipped on snow and slid about 100 feet into rocks, hitting her head and injuring her left lower leg. Schuster confirmed a possible broken leg. Additionally, he found several contusions on her legs and arms with no bleeding.

Two rangers stayed with her through the night, providing overnight gear and medical support, while rangers Fletcher and Zeilman short-roped her four companions down steep snow, rock, and ice to Garnet Meadows and then to the Lupine Meadows parking lot, arriving about 6:30 a.m. Six additional members of her group had previously descended to the parking area and were waiting there.

At 8 a.m. on July 18, the helicopter tried again to extract the patient, but the wind was again too high. Four additional rangers were then sent to her location from the valley with a snow-lowering litter, and the six rangers now on the scene lowered and carried the patient to Garnet Meadows in the litter, arriving about 1 p.m. Six trail crew members with a wheeled litter had been dispatched to the Meadows to assist in a carry-out from there. However, the wind briefly calmed, and at about 2 p.m., the helicopter was able to land, pick up the injured patient, and fly her to the rescue cache, where she was loaded into the park ambulance. (*Source: Grand Teton National Park Search and Rescue Report.*)

This large group was comprised of members of a foreign alpine club. They were poorly prepared even for a moderate mountain route like the Southwest Couloir. The group did not have enough ice axes or crampons for everyone, nor appropriate footwear or clothing for the conditions. (There often is extensive snow travel on this route in mid-July.) The less experienced members were not partnered or accompanied by experienced mountaineers. The Southwest Couloir is a route where a grade (3rd class) or description (it is often called a "hike" online) fails to convey the seriousness of a remote alpine climb. (*Sources: Grand Teton National Park and the Editors.*)

FALL, STRANDED | Off-Route on Descent
Grand Teton National Park, Middle Teton

On August 23, at about 3:30 p.m., rangers received a call from a 24-year-old-man who had summited the Middle Teton via the Southwest Couloir but on the descent quickly became lost. As he attempted to descend a gully above the Northwest Ice Couloir, he slipped on wet rock and slid about 80 feet before catching himself. With a bruised knee and cut leg, he ascended about 20 feet to a point where he became stuck and called rangers for help. In cold shade at nearly 12,800 feet, with inadequate clothing, he became mildly hypothermic.

A helicopter search located the stranded individual about 80 feet below and west of the Middle Teton's summit. In two separate flights, the helicopter flew two rangers on a 250-foot short-haul rope and inserted them onto the summit of the Middle Teton. Both were in position by about 6 p.m. The two rangers rappelled to the injured climber, lowered him a short distance, and placed him in a screamer suit. Ranger Ronczkowski and the patient were short-hauled to Lupine Meadows at just after 7 p.m. (*Source: Grand Teton National Park Search and Rescue Report.*)

ANALYSIS

In both this incident and the following report, climbers ascended the standard route on Middle Teton (the Southwest Couloir) to the summit and then got disoriented as soon as they started down. Both ended up deviating significantly from the correct descent—the route they had just climbed. On a peak like the Middle Teton, much of your day may be spent on well-beaten trails or an obvious ascent route, such as a snowfield with tracks or a gully with cairns. But the summit itself can be a surprisingly amorphous pile of rocks. As you exit the climbing route into the summit area, stop several times to look back and study the descent route from above, identifying landmarks. If the descent doesn't seem familiar or "right," backtrack to the top before it becomes too difficult and try again. (*Source: The Editors.*)

FALL ON SNOW, STRANDED | Off-Route on Descent
Grand Teton National Park, Middle Teton

At approximately 7:45 p.m. on September 7, Teton Interagency Dispatch transferred a call to ranger R. Schuster from a distressed 28-year-old female climber. She explained that she'd taken a 30-foot fall on snow while descending the Middle Teton and now was stuck, surrounded by steep walls, and unable to move up or down.

The woman and her partner had left Lupine Meadows at 8 a.m. with a plan to climb the Middle Teton via the Southwest Couloir. They became separated somewhere in the upper South Fork of Garnet Canyon at about 10:30. The woman continued up the Southwest Couloir, hoping to meet her partner along the route; however, unknown to her, the partner had descended into Garnet Canyon.

The woman summited the Middle Teton around 5 p.m. She

Location of a stranded climber in the South Couloir of Middle Teton. She had been attempting to descend the Southwest Couloir, far to the left. Storms and high wind prevented a quick rescue—she was extracted by helicopter about 19 hours after calling for help. *NPS Photo*

was extremely anxious and nervous being alone on the summit and confused about the descent route. After a few unsuccessful attempts at descending, she committed to a route in a general southwest direction. During the descent, she got off route in steep, loose terrain and eventually slipped on snow, slightly injuring her hands. She stopped on a small, exposed ledge and called 911 to request help.

She was not able to report her location accurately, and cell phone coordinates were inconsistent and unreliable. At 9:15 p.m., rangers Ronczkowski and Pearson left Lupine Meadows trailhead to attempt to locate the stranded climber and assist her down. At 12:34 a.m., the rangers made voice contact with her from the upper South Fork of Garnet Canyon, but due to faint calls and echoing canyon walls, they found it difficult to locate her position. Finally, at 2:47 a.m., the rangers located the headlamp of the stranded climber high on the peak in the South Couloir (well to climber's right of the Southwest Couloir). They attempted to climb the couloir to reach to her but determined it to be too dangerous in the dark. They decided to climb the Southwest Couloir to the summit and attempt to downclimb to her location. At 4:41 a.m., they reached the summit and soon decided to rest there and wait for first light to continue.

Over the next several hours, the rangers attempted to descend to the stranded climber's position and another team of rangers attempted to reach her by helicopter. At 8:14 a.m., following a reconnaissance flight, ranger Johnson was short-hauled into the climber's location from the helicopter. However, soon after Johnson was on scene, rain and snow showers moved into the area, delaying any further flights.

By early afternoon, after several unsuccessful helicopter extraction attempts in very poor weather conditions, rescuers were in position to begin a technical raise of the patient toward the summit of the Middle Teton. The first raise of Johnson and the patient was completed at about 1:15 p.m.

A small break in the weather could be seen coming shortly after 2 p.m., so the team again prepared for a short-haul extraction. After one false start due to icing conditions, ranger Johnson and the patient were successfully extracted at about 3 p.m. and delivered to Lupine Meadows, where she was treated for hypothermia and dehydration. (*Source: Grand Teton National Park Search and Rescue Report.*)

ANALYSIS
Like the climber in the report above, this person was alone on the summit of Middle Teton and got confused about the descent. Teton rangers encourage climbers to stick together—two heads are often better than one for route-finding decisions. In addition, she had left the trailhead at 8 a.m. and reached the summit late in the afternoon during the relatively short days of September—the pressure of oncoming nightfall may have contributed to her decision-making. (*Sources: Grand Teton National Park and the Editors.*)

HIT BY BOULDER WHILE SCRAMBLING
Grand Teton National Park, Death Canyon

Just after 5 p.m. on July 18, a climber made a 911 call reporting that his partner had been hit by a very large boulder; he then fell and sustained injuries to his back, foot, and hand. The two climbers had been planning to do Raven's Crack, near the mouth of Death Canyon, the next day, and the injured person, a 22-year-old male, had scrambled up a chimney (low 5th class) to scout the approach and collect water. While climbing back down, he dislodged some small rocks that were holding a large chockstone (reportedly "the size of a car"), which rolled into him and barely missed his partner. The climber fell about 20 feet and slid another 10 feet to the base of the chimney.

Based on the reported injuries and the location of the injured person, a helicopter with rangers on board and a ranger on foot were sent to investigate. At approximately 7 p.m., one ranger arrived on scene after hiking in. He requested a litter to package the patient, who had injuries to his back and extremities. Helicopter 35HX delivered the litter via short-haul, and then, at about 8:10 p.m., the helicopter returned to extract the patient. The injured person's partner hiked out on his own. (*Sources: National Park Service Search and Rescue Report and notes from the climber.*)

ANALYSIS
The injured climber provided some notes about what he had learned:
- Always carry a two-way satellite communication device, and don't hesitate to use the device when necessary.
- I was very cautious while ascending the couloir but not while descending. I assumed everything must be solid since I had climbed up without any issues.
- There was no reason to go up the couloir in the first place. It looked like something fun to climb with the reward of water. However, there was a stream 200 meters below our bivy site. I should have filled my water bottles there.
- Over time you can become numb to exposure and begin to ignore the risks of easy soloing. This accident has been a great reminder to always respect the alpine environment, no matter if you're 500 feet up a wall or doing an easy approach or descent. (*Source: Injured climber.*)

ROCKFALL
Grand Teton National Park, Gilkey Tower

At approximately 11:15 a.m. on August 31, a climber called 911 to report that he was with a 38-year-old man from another climbing party who had been injured by rockfall on Gilkey Tower and was unable to move under his own power. The caller was a solo climber making a traverse from the South Teton to Nez Perce. The injured man had been roped to two partners doing the same traverse. On Gilkey Tower, the solo climber was above the other group when a ledge he was standing on broke loose. The subsequent rockfall raked the three climbers below. Two of the partners managed to dodge the rocks, but a watermelon-size rock struck the 38-year-old man. The force of the impact knocked him off his stance, and he slid approximately 10 feet before being caught on belay by one of his partners. The solo climber descended to the injured man and helped assess his injuries, which included contusions, abrasions, and a large hematoma on his thigh. They determined that he needed a rescue.

At about 1:10 p.m., after a reconnaissance flight, ranger K. Kreis was short-hauled to the accident site. He assessed the injured climber and confirmed a short-haul extraction was warranted, and at 1:45 p.m., after splinting the injured leg for the short-haul, he and the injured man were extracted from Gilkey Tower and brought to Lupine Meadows. (*Source: National Park Service Search and Rescue Report.*)

ANALYSIS
On busy routes, each party must continuously monitor the position of other climbers to assess the potential for rockfall and other hazards. Although the exact circumstances in this case are not known, a good practice is for a faster party to ask if the others are in a good position before passing overhead, and for the trailing party to pause in a sheltered spot whenever someone passes. (*Source: The Editors.*)

FATAL FALL IN ATTEMPT TO ASSIST PARTNER
Wind River Range, Cirque of the Towers, Pingora Peak

On August 10, Zijah Kurtovic (63) fell to his death during an attempt on 11,889-foot Pingora Peak. While leading the final pitch (5.6) of a route on the east side of Pingora, his climbing partner (male, 67) fell 40 to 50 feet and suffered fractures to seven vertebrae, four ribs, and his right ankle, along with a hemothorax. Kurtovic secured his partner with a length of rope, as the man was unable to hold himself in place due to his injuries, and then apparently left the accident site to seek help. Neither he nor his partner had cell service or a SEND device to call for rescue. At some point, and likely while rappelling, Kurtovic fell.

Nearby climbers came to the aid of the injured partner, providing first aid and using their Garmin inReach to send an SOS and to communicate with search and rescue. Thanks to their efforts, the injured climber was successfully short-hauled from the peak that day by helicopter. His partner's body was recovered days later by Fremont County Search and Rescue. (*Sources: Jameson Harper (climber on the scene), Tip Top Search and Rescue, and media reports.*)

ANALYSIS

Although we do not have an account of what happened after Kurtovic secured his injured partner high on Pingora, the actions of the climbers who assisted should be noted. Activating search and rescue soon after an accident can make the difference between life and death. Staying calm, as these climbers did, not only assists the injured climber but also is essential to communicating the needed details to a search and rescue team.

When communicating with 911 dispatch or search and rescue, focus on providing a precise geographic location, including GPS coordinates and any terrain elements that might impede or complicate a rescue. Additionally, a detailed assessment of the climber's injuries (head to toe, with a focus on life-threatening factors) and any pertinent medical history will be helpful. Remember that communicating is a two-way street—listen to their instructions. In many cases, a SAR team member can walk you through helpful steps in an emergency and how to signal to responding SAR units. (*Source: The Editors.*)

HIGH ALTITUDE PULMONARY EDEMA
Wind River Range, Gannett Peak

On August 9, Darwin Day (64) was attempting to summit Gannett Peak to complete his goal of climbing the highest mountain in each of the Western states when he began to feel ill. It's not known how high Day and his climbing partner reached on the 13,804-foot peak. They decided to descend to Island Lake, at about 10,400 feet, but Day's condition continued to deteriorate. Rangers made contact with the party, and he was airlifted to a nearby hospital by Idaho Search and Rescue. Rescue workers were able to revive him, but he passed away three days later.

Gannett Peak as seen from Bonney Pass, during the approach from Island Lake. The 13,804-foot mountain is the highest peak in Wyoming. *Mark Thomas*

ANALYSIS

Although Day had climbed many mountains during his lifetime, including many that were higher than Gannett Peak, he had never experienced altitude illness. Based upon reports, the climber was experiencing high altitude pulmonary edema (HAPE). He and his partner took the correct action in immediately descending, as this is the gold standard for treatment of all altitude-related illnesses. The best method to prevent HAPE and other altitude illnesses is by adhering to a gradual ascent profile, especially a gradual increase in sleeping elevation. (*Sources: Mountain Project, media reports, and the Editors.*)

TOP-ROPE SOLO SYSTEM FAILURE

Vedauwoo, To the Moon Alice Area

On August 20, I (male, 26) drove up to the Voo for some after-work top-rope soloing. I set up a fixed line on To the Moon (5.10b/V0), a 35-foot crack with a bolted anchor that is often bouldered. I had not climbed the route before.

For soloing, I use a Kong Duck mini-ascender with a paracord sling around my neck to keep the device high on the fixed rope, prevent it from weighting the rope dynamically, and to keep it separate from my Petzl Microtraxion, which I use below the Duck as a backup. I placed both devices on the rope and tested that they were engaging properly. I was about to start climbing when I realized I had forgotten my crack gloves. I unclipped both devices from my harness and removed the paracord sling from my neck, leaving both devices attached to the rope, and walked over to my pack to get my gloves. Then I clipped back into the devices and put the sling around my neck. I did not recheck my system.

The route has a classic Vedauwoo start—the base of rock is overhung for the first ten feet or so. I struggled with the climbing, and I was fighting to keep the rope out of the crack where I was trying to jam. I probably weighted my system three or four times. At some point, I noticed the Kong Duck had slipped down the rope and was right on top of the Microtraxion, instead of higher on the rope as it should be.

I tried to correct this by holding onto the rope above the devices, so I could unweight them and try to get the system working properly. I pulled the Duck up the rope, then disengaged the cam on the Microtraxion and slid it back down the rope. When I reweighted the system, I fell about ten feet. My hand was on the rope, so I slid fairly slowly and received a minor rope burn, but was otherwise uninjured.

At the base of the route, I saw that the paracord had gotten tangled in the Duck, disabling its cam. It took me a few weeks to figure out why the Microtraxion had not held my weight (the Microtraxion was properly rigged). I am fairly certain that after I disengaged the cam on the Microtraxion, the disabled Duck slid back down the rope and held the Microtraxion open, so that neither device engaged.

ANALYSIS

Complacency and haste were the major factors in this accident. I had probably top-rope soloed around 50 to 60 pitches in Vedauwoo that summer and felt comfortable with the system, but was in a hurry to get some climbing in after work and failed to recheck my system when I clipped back into it.

I should have realized that my Duck was disabled and certainly not messed with both devices at the same time. Sometimes I tie backup knots in my rope, but in this situation I was so close to the ground that I didn't really have a chance to tie backups yet. Some people fix two separate lines and place one device on each line; this would have prevented my accident, but I find that with crack climbing, keeping one rope out of the crack is hard enough.

This accident was very minor, and I only share it because it could have been very serious under different circumstances. When climbing alone, it is important to always double-check your systems. (*Source: Anonymous and the Editors.*)

CANADA

GROUND FALL | Inadequate Protection
British Columbia, Squamish, Smoke Bluffs

On July 10, a climber was demonstrating a roped solo system to a friend while leading the route Libya Sucks (5.7). The climber was using a Grigri as his self-belay device. He placed a few pieces of protection low on the route, then stood up at a good stance and placed his next piece (a cam, size unknown) at chest height. He clipped the lead rope to this cam, then attempted to demonstrate that he could rest ("take") on the rope using his self-belay. However, the piece pulled out, and his earlier protection was too low to keep him from hitting the ground. He landed on his back and broke one vertebra.

ANALYSIS
The climber attributed the cam failure to the fact that the direction of pull on the piece was different than anticipated; he had placed and tested the cam in anticipation of a fall from above, but when he weighted it at the stance, the pull was outward. He also acknowledged it was a "poor placement." A general lesson from this incident is to back up a marginal piece if it is the only thing keeping you from hitting the ground or a ledge in the event of a fall. In addition, a Grigri is not recommended or approved by Petzl as a self-belay device. (*Sources: Facebook post from the climber and the Editors.*)

FALL ON ROCK | Inadequate Protection, Handhold Broke
British Columbia, Squamish, Stawamus Chief

On the morning of August 4, a 33-year-old man was leading the fourth pitch of Parallel Passages, a long 5.10 route in the North Walls area of Stawamus Chief. This highly experienced climber, with 5.13 trad routes under his belt, had free-soloed this route previously. There is a 5.4 scrambling section on the traversing fourth pitch, and the climber did not place any protection on this section. His belayer reported that a handhold broke and he tumbled approximately 25 meters, striking three ledges. His partner soloed up the lower part of the pitch (5.10a) to access the climber and wait for help with him. Other climbers arrived and were able to lower the patient to a ledge and administer first aid. The patient passed away before he could be long-lined off the cliff by helicopter, four hours after the accident. (*Sources: Rock and Ice magazine and other published reports.*)

ANALYSIS
Regardless of how easy the climbing might be or the abilities of the leader, the potential for a dangerous fall is always present. Familiarity with a route does not preclude the possibility of holds breaking or encountering wet or vegetated rock, or unforeseen hazards such as aggressive wasps. The merits of free-soloing a difficult pitch to administer first aid can be debated, but one maxim of performing rescues is to avoid unnecessary danger that might result in a secondary accident. (*Source: The Editors.*)

BELAYER PULLED INTO ROCK | Poor Position

British Columbia, Skaha Bluffs, Plum Wall

On March 23, my climbing partner and I were finishing our day of climbing on a 5.9 sport route called Sagging Bumline. It was a sunny day, we felt rested, and the climb was well within our limits. This is a 35-meter sport climb, and we were using a brand-new 70-meter rope. I was belaying my partner with an ATC. We were both wearing helmets, and I had approach shoes on.

Sagging Bumline is the sister climb to the very popular Plum Line (5.9) just to its left. Plum Line is notorious for accidents due to the length of the climb (35 meters), and various climbers have rappelled off the ends of their ropes or dropped their second. Therefore, a rappel station was added at a ledge approximately eight meters off the ground, reached by scrambling. This station allows climbers with a 60-meter rope to complete a second rappel or scramble to the ground. This ledge is also where you clip the first bolt of Sagging Bumline.

Below the ledge and slightly to the right is a large alcove or cave feature, which is directly under the first bolt of Sagging Bumline. We recognized that there was a risk of the belayer being pulled into the roof of the cave should the leader fall, and we decided to stand farther left under the first bolt of Plum Line.

We completed our safety check, and the leader cleanly led the first 30 meters of the route to the final bolt and crux move. He attempted to make the final clip but dropped the rope. As I began pulling in extra rope and trying to move into a squatting position to brace for a potential fall, the leader fell off. I was pulled off the ground approximately seven or eight meters, swung to the right toward the first bolt, and pulled into the wall. I bent my knees and put my feet up to brace for impact against the wall, but I was rotating slightly so my left foot made contact first. I heard a very loud cracking sound and knew I had broken my left leg.

As I hung off the ground, I maintained control of the brake rope and the lead climber hanging above. I began to call for help, and two climbers ran over to assist. I explained I had broken my leg and still had my lead climber on belay. I lowered myself to the ground, where the assisting party was able to enter the system and remove me safely. They then lowered the lead climber to the ground without incident.

One climber made cell phone contact with 911 and Penticton SAR while others splinted and elevated my broken left leg, and kept me warm and calm while the rescue team was assembled. A ground team from Penticton SAR attended the scene first. Due to the steep access and snow on the ground, the team decided that a helicopter lift would be the safest extraction method. At Penticton Hospital, I underwent surgery the next morning for a mid-shaft transverse tibia/fibula fracture. I was discharged four days later, and I am back climbing today.

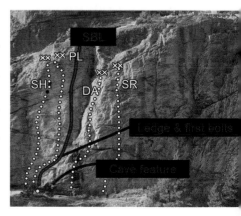

Accident scene at Skaha Bluffs. SBL is the Sagging Bumline route. Yellow dot marks the belayer's position below the adjacent Plum Line. *Hans Bauck*

ANALYSIS

Belayer positioning and a substantial weight difference between the leader and belayer were the main factors in this accident. I did not want to be under that roof if my partner fell, so I decided to stand farther left. Unfortunately, this meant there was a lot of extra rope out and I was pulled up and into a swing by the leader's fall. I still feel it was the right decision to stand further left because I might have broken my neck by hitting the roof instead.

A ground anchor might have prevented the dangerous swing. There were no good opportunities to build an anchor in the rock at the base, though a small tree nearby might have withstood the force of the swing. The other option would have been to scramble up to the ledge and tie into the intermediate anchor at the rappel station in order to belay the leader.

My climbing partner is 45 pounds heavier than I am, which is right on the limit of what is considered safe. To compensate for this, we could have used the Edelrid Ohm, which is clipped to the first bolt of sport climbs and reduces the force on the belayer. Prior to the leader falling, I was in the midst of pulling in extra slack, and I was not bracing in my harness, ready to catch him. I have caught him many times when I was better positioned, and I have never been pulled so far up or with such force.

I was using an ATC-style device to belay. Had I lost control of my brake hand, the leader would have fallen 30 meters. Since the accident, we have purchased a Petzl Grigri, an assisted-braking device that lowers the chances of dropping the lead climber in this type of incident. I also recommend wearing a helmet while belaying. If I had hit my head instead of my leg, I might have been knocked unconscious and dropped the leader. (*Source: Allison Beynon.*)

RAPPEL ANCHOR FAILURE | Sling Untied, Inexperience
British Columbia, Valhalla Provincial Park, Niselheim

On July 27, my climbing partner (female, 25) and I (male, 31) climbed the east ridge of Niselheim and then began descending the fourth-class northwest ridge. As we were scrambling down the ridge, my partner found a rappel anchor consisting of a single piece of webbing around a good horn with two carabiners attached. The webbing looked new and in good condition, and we assumed someone had recently rappelled from it. I flaked the rope and handed it to my partner. She passed the rope through the two carabiners and began to rappel.

The anchor sling came undone immediately under her weight, and my partner fell approximately five meters on slabby rock. I quickly scrambled down to meet her. We checked for injuries, and luckily she only had minor cuts on her right hand and a bruise on her right hip. I collected the rope, the webbing anchor, and the two carabiners. The sling had come untied during the rappel. I found the webbing with an overhand knot in each end of it.

ANALYSIS

I could not see the knot before my partner began to rappel, because she was blocking my view. My partner has never tied webbing and was unfamiliar with a water knot, used to join the ends of webbing. When inspecting sling anchors, it is important to evaluate not only the quality of the material but also the knots. When in doubt, double up the anchor with a fresh sling. Just because a previous party has rappelled off an anchor does not mean it's safe. (*Source: Anonymous climber.*)

EDITOR'S NOTE: *The person who left this anchor likely was attempting to tie a water knot or single fisherman's knot but instead simply threaded the tail of one overhand knot through the body of the overhand at the other end of the sling. If someone rappelled off this anchor prior to this accident, all that held the webbing in place was the pressure of the loaded sling against the horn, with the tail end of the webbing squeezed by the single overhand. The tail would have gradually worked loose or slipped free as pressure was released. Since the reporting climber quickly scrambled down to the fallen climber, both likely could have downclimbed to avoid this rappel. In many cases, careful scrambling or a quick belay is a more efficient way to descend short steps than rappelling, and often safer than relying on anchors of unknown provenance. If you encounter a dubious or damaged rappel anchor, dismantle or replace it to safeguard subsequent parties.*

Two climbers found this sling in situ while descending Niselheim. Shortly after the first climber began a short rappel, the improperly tied sling came undone and the climber fell.

AVALANCHE FATALITY | Poor Position, Weather
British Columbia, Mt. Stephen, Massey's

On Monday, March 11, a guided party of six climbers, consisting of two guides and four clients, climbed Massey's, the popular WI4 ice route near Field. This was the second day of a four-day waterfall ice climbing camp. On the previous day, the group had climbed at Haffner Creek.

Climbing as two roped teams, they ascended four pitches to the top of Massey's and then rappelled back to the base. Prior to leaving the area, the group gathered for a lesson on V-thread ice anchors. Just before 3 p.m., while they were standing at the base of the climb, a large, fast-moving avalanche that started high overhead ran down the climb and caught all of the climbers. Two were buried, one completely and another with her head and arm barely exposed. The climbers' packs, which were sitting on the ground nearby, were swept away and buried.

The guides immediately began searching. After determining that the partially buried victim was uninjured, they left her in place and concentrated on finding the missing person. Within two minutes, they had located her using an avalanche transceiver. She was buried under approximately 1.8 meters of snow. However, the guides were unable to dig effectively because all of their shovels and probes had been buried with the missing packs. Instead, they dug frantically with crampons and helmets.

The initiation of the avalanche had been witnessed by another guide from the same climbing camp who was near the parking lot. She immediately phoned one of

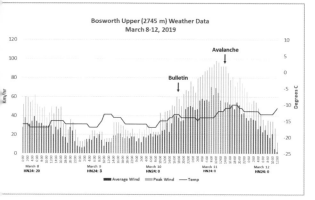

[Top] The northwest side of Mt. Stephen, one week after the avalanche. The face is an enormous snow collection zone that feeds directly onto the Massey's ice route (located in the gully in right center). [Bottom] Graph of accelerating wind speeds in the 30 hours before the Massey's avalanche. *Grant Statham / Parks Canada*

the guides on Massey's to warn of the impending avalanche and then began running the 1.8-kilometer approach to the climb, bringing rescue equipment. She contacted Parks Canada, then notified another guide working on an adjacent route. Upon her arrival at Massey's, she and the other guides were able to extricate the buried victim and start CPR, after a burial time of approximately 32 minutes. Parks Canada rescuers arrived on the scene at 3:45 p.m., took over the CPR, and then used a helicopter sling to transport the patient to a nearby ambulance. She was taken to hospital in Calgary, where she passed away.

ANALYSIS

Massey's is a 140-meter ice climb located in the run-out zone of a large avalanche path on the northwest side of Mt. Stephen. This path travels a linear distance of 2,400 meters from its top to the end of the run-out zone. The climb itself is rated Class 3 (complex) according to the Avalanche Terrain Exposure Scale (ATES).

This avalanche occurred at the end of a two-month spell of cold, dry weather in the Canadian Rockies. The snowpack had weakened considerably over this time and was comprised mostly of faceted grains with very little strength. The snowpack was at a tipping point where new snow and variable wind or temperature could change things immediately.

Parks Canada's avalanche bulletin for Monday, March 11, rated the avalanche danger as moderate in alpine areas and low at the treeline and below. The bulletin warned that the alpine and treeline avalanche danger would increase on Tuesday, March 12, "with the arrival of new snow and strong alpine winds Monday night."

The wind arrived early, ahead of the snow. Parks Canada's Bosworth Upper weather station, located 10 kilometers northeast of Massey's at an altitude of 2,745 meters, showed steadily increasing winds starting Sunday afternoon and reaching peak gusts of 98 kph (61 mph) by 10 a.m. on Monday (see chart). This wind combined with 20 centimeters of new snow from three days prior to produce significant wind loading in alpine areas overnight on Sunday and throughout the day on Monday. During this time, the alpine temperatures remained cold, rising from -17°C on Sunday morning to -11°C at the time of the incident on Monday.

The wind loading on March 11 overloaded the weak snowpack above Massey's, and a large natural avalanche released at approximately 2,500 meters above sea level. The avalanche traveled a linear distance of 1,500 meters, running over the climb (which is located below treeline), and stopped in the run-out zone below.

The climbers had grouped closely together for the V-thread lesson at the base of the climb when they were impacted by the avalanche. Despite receiving a warning phone call, the group had no time to react before they were struck. They had carried avalanche rescue equipment, but it was buried or swept away with their packs when the avalanche hit. (*Source: Grant Statham/Parks Canada.*)

RAPPEL ERROR | Clipped Only One Strand into Device
Alberta, Jasper National Park, Lost Boys Area

In midafternoon on May 30, rescue personnel responded to a report that a 63-year-old man had fallen from the top of Lost Boys. He was located at the base of Super Brant Man (5.10b), in between large boulders. The climber's rope, harness, carabiners, and belay device were in good condition. He had a daisy chain on his harness with which he likely had secured himself at the top of the route. The patient was not wearing a climbing helmet and had suffered head trauma. He was declared deceased at the scene.

ANALYSIS
Due to the configuration of the rope and technical gear, it was determined that this was a rappel failure. Only one rappel strand of the climbing rope was clipped through the belay device and carabiner attached to the belay loop of the climber's harness. With this setup, the patient weighted one strand of the rope and pulled the other half all the way through the anchor, resulting in a 20-meter fall. His climbing partner was at the base of the climb and could not have checked his setup.

In addition to the faulty rappel setup, the climber did not use a third-hand backup or wear a helmet (though neither likely would have prevented the tragic results of this accident). Always perform a bounce test after setting up your rappel system and before detaching your connection from the anchor. (*Sources: Jesse Milner, Parks Canada Rescue Technician and the Editors.*)

AVALANCHE | Fatigue, Failure to Heed Warning Signs
Alberta, Jasper National Park, Diadem Peak

Late on July 19, a group of three hiked to a bivouac below Diadem Peak. They arrived at 2 a.m. and slept for a few hours. The temperature overnight remained warm at around 4°C. A clearing trend was under way after a week of precipitation. The climbers' goal was the southeast face of Diadem Peak (3,371 meters/11,060 feet).

They departed camp at approximately 7:30 a.m. Shortly after the first direct sunlight reached the slopes, a small (size 1) loose wet avalanche ran down a drainage channel on the slope they were ascending. Since they were within meters of their intended traverse out of the couloir, they continued. Near the end of the long leftward traverse, one of the climbers felt the risk of another avalanche was too great, and she

Diadem Peak with the route followed by three climbers on the southeast face. (A) Site of first avalanche, originating in the widening of the couloir above. (B) Location of two climbers when the second avalanche occurred. (C) Point where the two climbers stopped after the slide. *Parks Canada*

decided to wait in the rocks for her companions to return. The two others continued into the next couloir. They were almost at the point where they would leave this feature when, they believe, they triggered a size 2 slab avalanche. They both were carried down the mountain.

One of the climbers remained on top of the debris throughout the slide (with some effort). Once they stopped moving, he excavated his partner, whose head and torso were buried. He then activated his Garmin inReach and radioed for help. Although initially unconscious, the second climber quickly regained his senses. (His helmet, which had been badly damaged during the avalanche, had likely saved his life.) Although suffering a broken ankle and a lacerated chest from his partner's crampons during the avalanche, the first climber was able to move his injured partner to a position that was less exposed to the danger of serac fall and provide information to rescuers. A rescue team responded, recovering all three climbers.

ANALYSIS

An unusually wet and cold summer had contributed to a lingering and unstable snowpack at the time of the accident. Precipitation gauges at Job Creek and Southesk showed that 25 to 38 mm fell between July 14 and July 20, with around 12 mm falling on July 19, the day before this incident. Furthermore, after cool temperatures on July 19 (and associated snowfall in the alpine), the freezing level spiked upward on July 20.

The Public Avalanche Bulletin for Jasper National Park issued May 13, 2019, which was valid until further notice, warned of spring conditions and stated, "Traveling early in the day is recommended, as conditions can change rapidly in short periods of time due to daytime warming" and "When the sun comes out, temperatures soar above freezing, or rain falls, expect wet loose avalanches and cornice failures. This is especially relevant in steep, high-consequence terrain, such as gully climbs...."

The climbers' late arrival at their bivy and their fatigue once there resulted in a late start. The warm overnight temperatures and cloudy skies had not produced the desired overnight freeze. These factors contributed to the increased avalanche danger on the day of the accident, and their exposure increased as the day warmed up. One of the trio, it appears, had come to this conclusion but was unable to deter her companions.

The group was not carrying avalanche beacons, shovels, or probes. However, all the group members carried good communication tools, which resulted in rapid and effective notification of Jasper's rescue team. (*Source: Rupert Wedgewood, Jasper National Park Visitor Safety.*)

LONG FALL ON ICE | Unclipped from Anchor
Alberta, Banff National Park, Icefields Parkway

Two climbers (male, 33, and female, 36) left their car at 5 a.m. on March 25, planning to climb Polar Circus, a long ice route above the Icefields Parkway. The risk of an avalanche was rated "moderate," and during the previous evening the team had discussed trying to get up and down the route by about noon in order to minimize exposure to wet slab avalanches.

Approach conditions were slow, with crusty post-holing, but the approach ice pitches went quickly, and the pair reached the start of the guidebook pitches at about 7 a.m. After guidebook pitches one through three, there was another long, slow stretch of post-holing to get to the upper tiers.

Climber 1 attempted to link pitches four and five but came up short of the bolted belay. This long pitch took just over an hour to lead. Climber 2 then led a short segment of ice and slogged through snow to reach the belay atop pitch five. When the first climber arrived, she pointed out that it was nearly 11 a.m. and the slopes above the climb were now in the sun. She indicated the team should turn back, as per the previous evening's conversation. Climber 1 responded that the team was "two pitches from the top" (not true) and he "didn't come to Canada to turn back now." He started up pitch six, climbing quickly and placing minimal protection. He attempted to link pitches six and seven with their 60-meter ropes but did not reach the belay stance, and the belayer declined to simul-climb due to the lack of protection. Therefore, the leader built a belay one bulge below the snow ledge that marks the top of pitch seven. The anchor had no ice screws, using only the leader's ice tools.

Climber 2 followed the pitch and continued up past Climber 1's belay onto the snow ledge. She found the two-bolt anchor, clipped her belay device to an equalized sling, and began to pull up the ropes. She felt resistance and inserted the ropes into the belay device. Her partner then yelled, "They're tangled." Climber 2 continued to pull up rope until she had about six to eight feet of slack in her hands. Meanwhile, her partner had gotten uncomfortable at his hanging belay, and he unclipped from his anchor and stepped up to reach the tangled ropes. After Climber 2 pulled up a few more feet of rope, her partner's feet suddenly blew and he fell about 50 feet because of the slack still in the rope tangle. He stopped on a sloping ledge. Up top, his partner tried to hold the ropes in her hands, but they burned through her gloves until her partner weighted the belay device clipped to the anchor.

Climber 2 yelled down to her partner, but he was unresponsive, so she escaped the belay and began to descend the unweighted strand of their half ropes. However, she soon realized there was a massive core shot in the rope, so

Upper pitches of Polar Circus: (1) Climber 2's belay. (2) Climber's 1's stance. (3) Location of Climber 1 after his fall.

she stopped and tied off the damaged rope with an overhand on a bight. She could now see Climber 1, and she coached him through building a screw anchor and unweighting his rope. She then reascended to the anchor using prusiks and prepared to rappel, using a knot block so she could descend the single undamaged rope and pull it down with the core-shot strand. In similar fashion, the team descended the rest of the route with 11 rappels and post-holing. They made it back to the car by about 6:30 p.m. Climber 1 had a possible concussion, a fracture in one arm, and a possible back injury.

ANALYSIS

Climber 1 (the climber who fell): "My comfort in such terrain led to complacency, the most dangerous thing of all. Under no circumstances should one ever unclip from an anchor until they are on belay."

Climber 2: "Clear communication between partners is a safety concern. Turn-around times and belay expectations should be discussed and agreed to before "summit fever" takes effect. In addition, any climber embarking on long, remote climbs should not only be knowledgeable in self-rescue but also practice those techniques regularly, so that they can perform without hesitation in the event of an accident." (*Report source: Climber 2.*)

AVALANCHE

Alberta, Banff National Park, Howse Peak

The following report is based on the photographic record and equipment found with Hansjörg Auer, David Lama, and Jess Roskelley after an accident on April 16 on the east face of Howse Peak. Jess' iPhone was found on him at the base of the face. The phone provided exact time, altitude, and GPS locations from each of his photos, which not only proved they made the summit of the 3,295-meter peak, but also gave clues to the location of their route, a substantial new variation of the climb M-16, and the nature of their accident.

On my second trip (of three) to the accident site, on June 2, we found David Lama's GoPro and Hansjörg Auer's camera, both with informative photos. Using Jess' iPhone as the control for time and location, I sequenced the photos into a time line. The evidence shows they climbed the east face of Howse from their camp at the base to the summit (an altitude gain of 1,340 meters) in less than seven hours. Their ascent is a tribute to their strength, talent, and tenacity. Their deaths prove once again, though, that the mountain passes final judgment on success or failure.

The three men, all members of the North Face athlete team, arrived in Canmore the first week in April. They quickly made ascents of Andromeda Strain and Neme-sis, and then, on April 15, the three headed for Howse Peak. After an eight-kilometer ski approach, they camped below the east face. That evening, Hansjörg took several photos of small powder snow avalanches sweeping their intended route.

The route they followed the next day started up M-16, a difficult mixed climb with only one previous ascent (1999), then began a series of leftward traverses on some previously unclimbed and difficult terrain. Eventually they reached a large, concave snow basin above a waterfall route known as Life by the Drop. Ankle-deep in sun-warmed snow, Jess took the lead up the moderate snow basin to reach the southwest ridge. After more mixed climbing along the ridge, the three reached the summit prior to 12:41 p.m. The sun was shining, but a few clouds were starting to move in.

Sometime after Jess' summit photo taken at 12:44 p.m., the three climbers began their descent. At 1:27 p.m., Hansjörg took the last photo found on any of the three cameras. The photo is probably of David at the bottom of their rappel from the ridge into the snow basin.

Just before 2 p.m., Quentin Roberts, an alpinist living in Canmore, stopped along the Icefields Parkway on his way back from a climb farther north to examine the routes on Howse Peak. As he and his partner stood looking at the east face, an avalanche swept the basin above the route Life by the Drop and billowed onto the glacier at the bottom of the face. They did not know that Hansjörg, David, and Jess were on the face at the time. A massive snow cloud formed at the bottom of the face. It was 1:58 p.m., 31 minutes after the three climbers had entered the basin.

Jess always phoned in after a climb, and he had told Allison, his wife, they would be out of the mountains that night. If he was unable to phone, he would have texted his position to her on his Garmin inReach device. No message came. At 7:30 a.m. on April 17, I called Royal Canadian Mounted Police dispatch, which connected me

The line climbed on the east face of Howse Peak on April 16. The climbers were avalanched from the obvious snow bowl near the top during their descent from the summit. *Parks Canada*

with a Parks Canada ranger. They immediately dispatched a ranger to the Waterfowl Lakes parking lot to see if Jess' truck was still there. It was.

A Parks Canada search and rescue team was flown by helicopter to the base of Howse Peak. Clouds now blanketed the mountain. As they flew toward the avalanche cones at the bottom of the face, the rangers were drawn to a dark shadow in the snow. A close inspection from the helicopter indicated at least one climber was buried halfway up the large avalanche cone below Life by the Drop.

Avalanche conditions were extreme, so the SAR team decided not to put rescuers on the ground. Because the climbers were not wearing transceivers, the team tossed two large fluorescent traffic cones and two avalanche beacons where the climber(s) were located and then departed. For the next four days, bad weather prevented search and rescue or recovery efforts.

On April 20, the weather was clear and sunny. A SAR team on board a helicopter searched up and down the mountain, looking for signs of survivors. Nothing was seen after a meticulous search. They then concentrated their efforts on recovery. The SAR team, plus a recovery dog and her handler, were flown to a staging area below the face. They made one sortie to probe the avalanche cone, with the SAR members working while attached to the long line below the helicopter, but after four days of snow and wind, they could not locate the climbers. As the avalanche danger increased and the light became poor, the search operation was suspended for the day.

The following day, rangers returned to the site, and after two unsuccesful attempts to probe for the climbers, the pilot long-lined the dog and her handler into the site, and the dog soon located one of the climbers. The rangers were flown back to dig out the three climbers, who were close together. The rangers quickly cut their two 50-meter ropes in as many as 30 places to free the climbers from the ice and each other. They were then long-lined to the staging area and eventually to ambulances waiting on the highway.

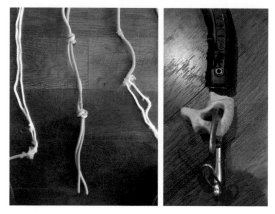

Ropes and an ice tool damaged in the avalanche incident on Howes Peak. *Roskelley Collection*

ANALYSIS

More likely than not, an avalanche swept the climbers to their deaths. Evidence from the ropes and equipment suggests the climbers did not rope up once they had rappelled into the basin. As competent as they all were, they would have plunge-stepped quickly down the slope toward the traverse leading back to the first part of their ascent line.

When found, their two ropes were still joined for rappelling with an overhand knot and long tails backed up with a second overhand. In addition, there were two loops formed with overhand knots. After the ropes were pulled from the rappel into the basin, one of the climbers, most likely Jess, must have located the centers of the two ropes and then tied an overhand with a 20-inch loop. I believe that Jess, who had by far the most rope wrapped around him when the climbers were found, put this big loop over his shoulder and then loop-coiled the rest of the two ropes over his neck. He must have planned to carry them across the traverse and down to the next rappel.

I think Jess also tied the fourth knot, a standard-size overhand on a bight on two strands, approximately 21 feet below the center loop, and clipped this loop to a carabiner attached to the ferrule on one of his tools, possibly as a moveable anchor as he descended. There's strong evidence that Jess had placed his ice tool with significant effort, with the loop attached, prior to the avalanche reaching them. The force snapped the ferrule of his tool at the point where it's pinned to the shaft, and the carabiner through the ferrule was twisted, with the gate sprung permanently open. The overhand knots with loops were pulled so tight it's like they were woven of steel.

In conclusion, it's unlikely the accident was caused by a fall, because the evidence shows they were unroped and, if one had fallen, he likely wouldn't have taken out the others. All the evidence indicates they were swept to their deaths in that short window from the time they dropped into the basin and the photo from the highway confirmed an avalanche. It doesn't bring them back into our arms, but the story of their last climb gives some closure to families and friends. (*Source: John Roskelley.*)

MÉXICO

RAPPEL ERROR | Uneven Ropes, No Stopper Knots
Nuevo León, El Potrero Chico

Brad Gobright, 31, one of the best-known big-wall climbers and soloists in North America, died in a rappelling accident at El Potrero Chico on November 27. Gobright and his climbing partner for the day (male, 26) had teamed up to attempt El Sendero Luminoso, a 15-pitch limestone route. They had not climbed together before.

The two successfully climbed the 5.12+ route, with Gobright onsighting the entire climb. To descend, they planned to simul-rappel the route from bolted anchors, using a single 80-meter rope. The descent went smoothly until midafternoon, when they reached a stance above the large bivy ledge on top of pitch five. Realizing they did not have enough rope to reach this ledge in one rappel, they decided to do two shorter rappels.

After the first rappel, the two prepared for a short rappel to the big ledge below. According to accounts provided by Gobright's partner, they did not pull the rappel rope all the way to the middle mark at the anchor, because it looked obvious they had enough rope out on both sides. One end of the rope could be seen on the ledge below, while the other strand (Gobright's side) was tangled in bushes below them.

As on the previous rappels, the two began descending together, counter-balancing each other's weight in a simul-rappel. Gobright said he would untangle the rope from the bushes en route. Suddenly, both men began dropping. The partner fell through some bushes and onto the ledge, without tumbling off the far side. Gobright continued falling and did not survive.

ANALYSIS
The evidence in published accounts strongly suggests the rope ends were not even and that the strand on Gobright's side was too short to reach the ledge. This fact was hidden by the bushes in which the rope was tangled, and he did not see the problem until the rope end passed through his rappel device.

The climbers were not using stopper knots in the ends of the rope. This was likely a conscious decision, because the many rock flakes, bushes, and cacti along this 1,500-foot descent could snag a rappel rope, and stopper knots can make ropes more prone to snagging, especially if there is any wind. However, it is also possible to keep the rope ends with you as you rappel (or one end with each climber in the case of simul-rappelling) to maintain control of the ends. If these two climbers had tied stopper knots, it's very unlikely this fatal accident would have occurred.

In simul-rappelling, when one climber unweights the rope prematurely, the other will drop, and this was the case for Gobright's partner. When he landed on the ledge, his rappel device and third-hand backup were still connected to the rope, which pulled through the anchor and dropped to the ledge after him. The partner was extremely lucky to land on one of the few sizable ledges on this entire route. He was able to descend with the assistance of other climbers. (*Sources: Media reports and the Editors.*)

TABLES

TABLE I: REPORTED CLIMBING ACCIDENTS

Year	Number of Accidents Reported		Total Persons Involved		Injured		Fatalities	
	USA	CAN	USA	CAN	USA	CAN	USA	CAN
1951	15	n/a	22	n/a	11	n/a	3	n/a
1952	31	n/a	35	n/a	17	n/a	13	n/a
1953	24	n/a	27	n/a	12	n/a	12	n/a
1954	31	n/a	41	n/a	31	n/a	8	n/a
1955	34	n/a	39	n/a	28	n/a	6	n/a
1956	46	n/a	72	n/a	54	n/a	13	n/a
1957	45	n/a	53	n/a	28	n/a	18	n/a
1958	32	n/a	39	n/a	23	n/a	11	n/a
1959	42	2	56	2	31	0	19	2
1960	47	4	64	12	37	8	19	4
1961	49	9	61	14	45	10	14	4
1962	71	1	90	1	64	0	19	1
1963	68	11	79	12	47	10	19	2
1964	53	11	65	16	44	10	14	3
1965	72	0	90	0	59	0	21	0
1966	67	7	80	9	52	6	16	3
1967	74	10	110	14	63	7	33	5
1968	70	13	87	19	43	12	27	5
1969	94	11	125	17	66	9	29	2
1970	129	11	174	11	88	5	15	5
1971	110	17	138	29	76	11	31	7
1972	141	29	184	42	98	17	49	13
1973	108	6	131	6	85	4	36	2
1974	96	7	177	50	75	1	26	5
1975	78	7	158	22	66	8	19	2
1976	137	16	303	31	210	9	53	6
1977	121	30	277	49	106	21	32	11
1978	118	17	221	19	85	6	42	10
1979	100	36	137	54	83	17	40	19
1980	191	29	295	85	124	26	33	8
1981	97	43	223	119	80	39	39	6
1982	140	48	305	126	120	43	24	14
1983	187	29	442	76	169	26	37	7

Year	Number of Accidents Reported		Total Persons Involved		Injured		Fatalities	
	USA	CAN	USA	CAN	USA	CAN	USA	CAN
1984	182	26	459	63	174	15	26	6
1985	195	27	403	62	190	22	17	3
1986	203	31	406	80	182	25	37	14
1987	192	25	377	79	140	23	32	9
1988	156	18	288	44	155	18	24	4
1989	141	18	272	36	124	11	17	9
1990	136	25	245	50	125	24	24	4
1991	169	20	302	66	147	11	18	6
1992	175	17	351	45	144	11	43	6
1993	132	27	274	50	121	17	21	1
1994	158	25	335	58	131	25	27	5
1995	168	24	353	50	134	18	37	7
1996	139	28	261	59	100	16	31	6
1997	158	35	323	87	148	24	31	13
1998	138	24	281	55	138	18	20	1
1999	123	29	248	69	91	20	17	10
2000	150	23	301	36	121	23	24	7
2001	150	22	276	47	138	14	16	2
2002	139	27	295	29	105	23	34	6
2003	118	29	231	32	105	22	18	6
2004	160	35	311	30	140	16	35	14
2005	111	19	176	41	85	14	34	7
2006	109	n/a	227	n/a	89	n/a	21	n/a
2007	113	n/a	211	n/a	95	n/a	15	n/a
2008	112	n/a	203	n/a	96	n/a	19	n/a
2009	126	n/a	240	n/a	112	n/a	23	n/a
2010	185	n/a	389	n/a	151	n/a	34	n/a
2011	157	n/a	348	n/a	109	n/a	29	n/a
2012	140	15	309	36	121	12	30	2
2013	143	11	283	24	100	5	21	4
2014	112	10	170	19	89	8	28	1
2015	173	20	258	52	111	16	37	4
2016	175	23	302	58	134	17	32	6
2017	162	24	n/a	n/a	116	19	34	2
2018	187	17	n/a	n/a	198	12	17	5
2019	202	18	n/a	n/a	148	12	31	9
TOTAL	8,207	1,096	n/a	n/a	6,827	816	1,744	325

TABLE II: REPORTED ACCIDENTS BY LOCATION

Geographic Districts	1951–2018 Number of Accidents	Deaths	2019 Number of Accidents	Deaths	Injured
Canada*					
Alberta	590	154	7	5	5
British Columbia	353	131	9	4	5
Yukon Territory	44	28			
New Brunswick	1	0			
Ontario	42	9	1	0	1
Québec	33	10	1		1
East Arctic	8	2			
West Arctic	2	2			
United States					
Alaska	650	226	16	2	12
Arizona, Nevada, Texas	141	26	5	0	5
Atlantic–North	1257	165	28	2	4
Atlantic–South	263	44	27	2	25
California	1630	344	43	8	34
Central	149	19	0	0	0
Colorado	1031	258	35	6	28
Montana, Idaho, South Dakota	104	41	10	4	7
Oregon	289	133	9	1	6
Utah, New Mex.	253	76	11	2	8
Washington	2073	353	6	2	9
Wyoming	667	164	12	2	10

TABLE III: REPORTED ACCIDENTS BY CAUSE

	1951–2018 USA	*1959–2018 CAN	2019 USA	2019 CAN
Terrain				
Rock	5610	605	155	13
Snow	2769	384	44	2
Ice	324	28	2	3
River	25	3	1	0
Unknown	26	11	0	0

	1951–2018 USA	*1959–2018 CAN	2019 USA	2019 CAN
Ascent or Descent				
Ascent	4448	650	106	12
Descent	1537	418	71	4
Unknown	369	18	17	1
Other[1]	51	5	8	1
Immediate Cause				
Fall or slip on rock	4293	326	81	7
Fall on snow or ice	1230	225	22	2
Falling rock, ice, or object	726	154	11	1
Exceeding abilities / Inexperience	612	36	3	0
Illness[2]	472	28	0	0
Stranded / Lost	451	67	14	0
Avalanche	339	140	2	3
Rappel Failure / Error[3]	439	61	18	2
Lowering Error[7]	29	2	10	1
Exposure	290	14	1	0
Loss of control / Glissade	248	18	1	0
Nut / cam pulled out	298	11	0	0
Failure to follow route	259	36	3	0
Fall into crevasse / moat	197	52	1	0
Faulty use of crampons	128	7	0	0
Piton / ice screw pulled out	95	13	0	0
Ascending too fast	82	0	6	0
Skiing[4]	85	16	6	0
Lightning	68	7	1	0
Equipment failure	18	3	1	0
Other[5]	640	43	7	0
Unknown	103	12	14	2
Contributory Causes				
Climbing unroped	1123	176	11	2
Exceeding abilities / Inexperience	1099	209	22	0
Placed no / inadequate protection	966	112	0	3
Inadequate equipment / clothing	794	78	0	0
Weather	551	82	5	2
Climbing alone	480	74	2	0
No helmet	406	77	10	0
Inadequate belay[6]	317	30	14	0
Nut / cam pulled out	275	36	14	1

	1951–2018 USA	*1959–2018 CAN	2019 USA	2019 CAN
Poor position	263	32	13	4
Darkness	194	23	1	0
Party separated	143	12	3	0
Loose rock / failure to test holds	145	53	8	1
Piton / ice screw pulled out	88	15	0	0
Failed to follow directions / route	136	20	14	0
Exposure	68	16	2	0
Illness[2]	49	10	0	0
Equipment failure	26	7	2	1
Other[5]	335	104	19	0
Age of Individuals				
Under 15	1252	12	1	0
15-20	1366	204	9	2
21-25	1669	262	34	1
26-30	1589	218	32	3
31-35	2204	19	28	4
36-50	3597	147	33	3
Over 50	469	37	27	2
Unknown	2437	622	59	6
Sex[7]				
Male	523	63	149	17
Female	143	13	50	4
Not known	126	18	24	0
Experience Level				
None/Little	1988	309	30	0
Moderate (1 to 3 years)	1870	365	37	2
Experienced	2622	511	78	10
Unknown	2863	622	78	9
Month				
January	283	28	1	0
February	267	62	4	1
March	411	79	6	3
April	514	45	12	1
May	1086	70	22	2
June	1349	84	33	2
July	2170	275	26	5

	1951–2018 USA	*1959–2018 CAN	2019 USA	2019 CAN
August	1243	211	30	4
September	2103	84	18	0
October	556	44	14	0
November	269	25	11	0
December	144	28	2	0
Unknown	85	3	23	0
Type of Injury/Illness (Data since 1984)				
Fracture	1841	260	71	8
Laceration	902	86	17	4
Abrasion	457	80	19	0
Bruise	629	90	16	1
Sprain / strain	505	38	10	0
Head injury/traumatic brain injury	399	36	35	4
Hypothermia	187	20	3	0
Frostbite	163	13	4	0
Dislocation	185	16	8	1
Puncture	64	14	3	0
Acute mountain sickness	55	0	2	0
HAPE	97	1	4	0
HACE	40	1	1	0
Other[8]	488	64	25	1
None	433	207	10	0

[N.B.] Data change: The 1986 and 1997 editions had some repeat data from previous years. The corrections are reflected in the cumulative data.

* No Canada data from 2006–2011; Includes new data from 2012–2019

[1] Some reported accidents happen when climbers are at the top or bottom of a route or (rarely) during an approach or in camp. This category was created in 2001. The category "unknown" is primarily because of solo climbers.
[2] These are illnesses/injuries that led directly or indirectly to an accident, such as HAPE.
[3] These include anchor failure, uneven ropes, no knots in rope ends, pendulum swings, and attaching device incorrectly. Prior years' data included some lowering errors.
[4] This category covers ski mountaineering. Backcountry ski touring or snowshoeing incidents, including those involving avalanches, are not counted in these tables.
[5] These include collapse of cliffline, fall from above while looking for a rappel anchor, fall from a Tyrolean traverse, prosthetic leg caught in crack, failure to engage top-rope solo device, and fall onto tree branch.
[6] These include miscommunication and ineffective belay.
[7] Categories introduced in 2016. The lowering errors include rope too short, miscommunication, and no knot in rope end.
[8] These include lightning injuries, rope burns, torn aorta, ruptured achilles tendon, and others.

Note: Injuries are counted only once in each category for a given incident. For example, an accident that results in three broken bones will only be listed once under "Fracture."

MOUNTAIN
RESCUE
ASSOCIATION

We Never Charge for Rescue

CLIMBERS HELPING CLIMBERS SINCE 1959.

MRA member Rocky Mountain Rescue
Group in action at Eldorado Canyon,
Colorado. Photo by Alison Sheets.

Courage. Commitment. Compassion.

www.mra.org